COACHING
FOR
FATHERHOOD

COACHING
FOR
FATHERHOOD

Teaching Men New Life Roles

By Lewis Epstein

New Horizon Press   Far Hills, NJ

Requests for permission should be addressed to:
New Horizon Press
P.O. Box 669
Far Hills, NJ 07931

Epstein, Lewis
    Coaching for Fatherhood: Teaching Men New Life Roles .

Library of Congress Catalog Card Number: Pending

ISBN: 0-88282-144-X

New Horizon Press

Manufactured in the U.S.A.

2000 1999 1998 1997 1996 / 5 4 3 2 1

Dedicated to Carl Bryant, mentor and friend,
and
to my family: past present, and future.

AUTHOR'S NOTE

This book is based on both my research and extensive interviews. In order to protect the identity of others, I have changed people's names and identifying characteristics. The conversations portrayed in this book have been reconstructed.

ACKNOWLEDGMENTS

I wish to thank many people for their support and help in writing this book. First, to my wife, Michelle, for opening my eyes to what it means to be a parent. I also wish to thank my children, Julie and Hannah, for their patience and understanding while I was more involved in writing than I was in their daily lives.

Special thanks to James Donnelly for his steadfast support and important advice. Special thanks also to Nydia Garcia Preto and other members of the staff of the Family Institute of New Jersey.

I want to express my gratitude to my mother, my sister, my aunt, and all of my cousins who gave me the information about my family without which I could never have written this book.

Thanks are also extended to the many men whom I interviewed about their relationships with their fathers and to my clients who allowed me to include aspects of their sessions in my text.

Certain writers in the area of family therapy and fathering have been influential in shaping my interest and thought. Among these are Murray Bowen, Michael Kerr, Harriet Goldhor Lerner, and Robert Pasick.

Thanks are also extended to the men from my men's groups over the past twenty-five years, who have had a powerful impact on my life and my fathering.

CONTENTS

INTRODUCTION

O UR SOCIETY IS IN a state of crisis. Not only do we feel concerns about the economy, the environment, and education, but social problems abound. Homelessness, drug and alcohol abuse, teenage pregnancy, teenage suicide, divorce, and domestic violence are found throughout America and many other countries. Most of these social ills are being treated by trained personnel working for government and private agencies, without much success. I think this is because we have not sufficiently attacked the underlying cause, which I believe is the absence of the father in many homes.

We hear about the arrest of a "deadbeat dad" on the news, and we find ourselves cheering the capture of this socially irresponsible man. While we are glad that he will finally have to make his child support payments, we may also recognize him as a product of our times. The deadbeat dad is one example of the diminished role and status of fathers in our society.

Dad's absence may be the result of divorce, separation, illegitimacy, or death, or it may be the absence of a father actually living with his family but distanced from his children by his inability to connect with them emotionally.

We are a people in search of a new concept of fatherhood. As a family counselor, I have talked to quite a few men over the years and have found that many of them are searching for new ways to handle the pressures of being men. They are not always sure about what is being asked of them by their families and society. Nor are they sure who they are supposed to be. If men are supposed to be more than just breadwinners like their fathers, then what more is expected of them? If men are now expected to be more intimate partners with their wives and more involved parents than their own fathers, where and how can they develop these qualities or acquire the necessary skills?

From my experience, I have found that the problem many men have in adapting to the pressures of being husbands and parents is rooted in the love and nurturing they did or did not receive in their family and in their relationships with their own fathers.

Many of us did not have the kind of father we would have needed in order to become the kind of man we would like to be. During the past decade, much has been written and spoken about the pain of "lost sons" and a "father hunger" that reflects a need for masculine attention that many of us never received as children. During the 1980s the poet Robert Bly led men into the woods for what he called "wildmen gatherings." The purpose of these meetings was to try to get men to reconnect with their missing fathers and to find a "deep masculinity." In a similar effort, the minister/psychotherapist John Bradshaw tried to get us to connect with our "inner child." Many men who attended these gatherings and workshops found that they had intense experiences while with the group but that these emotions failed to carry over into their daily lives. The pain from the missing father had been correctly diagnosed but often the prescribed remedy worked only briefly or not at all.

In this book I describe the problems that cause men pain in their relationships and prescribe a method by which men can return to the source of their original pain in order to understand

and resolve it. If followed conscientiously, the program produces permanent change. It has worked for me and for many of the men whom I have coached into new and more productive ways of relating to themselves and others.

Coaching for Fatherhood focuses on six types of fathers for whom these coaching techniques have proven greatly effective:

1) THE FATHER WHO IS THE "OUTSIDER" IN HIS FAMILY
   Many fathers and husbands are told by their wives and children that they are "too removed," "not available enough," or "always at work." This father may feel that he is fulfilling his obligations by being a good breadwinner. He may be puzzled and hurt that his family expects more from him. With coaching, this father can become a true insider in the family group.

2) THE FATHER WHO BECOMES TOO ANGRY
   I used to be a father who expressed too much anger. My anger kept other family members from getting close to me. Coaching helped me and others like me to resolve this common emotional problem that many fathers face.

3) THE SOCIALLY ISOLATED FATHER
   The isolated father has little or no network of friends or relatives with whom he maintains personal contact. He allows his partner to become the "family switchboard" and the "social secretary" in charge of all the couple's relation-ships. Men like this who keep their relationships at arm's length are still paying the price for the emotional distance they experienced with their own mothers and fathers. The process of reconnecting with one's first family is a central focus of the coaching offered in this book.

4) THE FATHER WHO "UNDERFUNCTIONS" IN THE HOME
   The underfunctioning father often depends on his wife to take care of all his children's needs. While he may be

highly successful at work, this father appears inept and dull at home. He runs the risk of abandoning his children in important ways, and he perpetuates the idea that fathers are second class family members. Coaching can turn this father into a full participant in his family group.

5) THE FATHER WHO HAS DIFFICULTY TAKING A POSITION
Many fathers leave the parental decision making to their wives. These men feel that their wives know more about their children's lives anyway, and they want to avoid conflict if they can. Coaching provides an approach to help fathers get over their lack of decisiveness in family life and shows fathers how to develop a stronger sense of themselves and their roles.

6) THE ESTRANGED FATHER
The father who, because of divorce or separation, is no longer part of the original family group but is still a parent to his children.

The problems that I present are not only those of other men. They are issues that I have worked on in my own family and with which I have struggled for a long time. The method of change presented in this book teaches men to employ skills that males have traditionally been taught since childhood and reapply them to the complicated tasks of adult life. Strategic moves and well-thought-out and constructed game plans are the key ingredients in this powerful method of self-change. Those who are willing to take courageous steps in a new direction and break old family "rules" will create new patterns of behavior for their fathering roles which benefit both themselves and the important people in their lives.

1

FATHERS AND THE EMOTIONAL VOID

Life for most boys and for many men is a frustrating search
for the lost father who has not yet offered protection, provision,
nurturing, modeling, or especially anointment.

Frank Pittman, *Man Enough*

THIS BOOK IS ABOUT men and the process of change. But meaningful change can only occur when we understand the nature
and magnitude of the problems we face. We have inherited from
the past a father-hungry society which I see as the root of many
of today's deepest societal ills. With increased understanding and
hard work, our generation may be able to correct the mistakes of
the past, overcome the inadequate nurturing in our own lives, and
reestablish the nurturing process with our children.

Most of the men I have known through my role as a family counselor have family histories in which their fathers were
often absent, underfunctioning, or weak. There is a type of fissure
running through their lives that I call the "emotional void." Like
them, all of my life I have had a sense that something vital was

missing from my own family history, but it was not until I began speaking with other men that I became aware of the depth of the loss.

One of my clients is Dan Kelly, a fireman from an Irish working class family. I met him in a men's group I joined about five years ago, and I learned a great deal about his life. Dan had a hard time setting limits with his children, especially in knowing where their needs ended and his began. He was also aware that he probably should have left the fire department years ago, because by skill and inclination he wanted to become a family counselor. Yet he remained in a job he did not like out of loyalty to a mysterious family rule that he has never figured out. All the males in his family wore uniforms to work. Dan's father, the member of the family who could do no wrong, was a policeman and so were his brother and his uncle.

Although Dan's father was hardly ever at home—he always worked the second shift—his impact on Dan's life was profound. Dan has one memory of his father that stands out. When Dan was about seven years old, he got out of bed at about midnight and passed the kitchen on the way to the bathroom. The room was dark except for the glow of a cigarette and the smell of coffee that John Kelly sipped from a mug. "Hiya, Danny," he said and looked away. This was the only communication between father and son that week. Back in bed in the darkness, Dan thought about his father. Daddy in uniform. Dad the outsider. Dad the observer. Dad the perfect one. Dad who sat at wedding parties at the end of the bar watching others get drunk while never himself losing control for a second. The family white knight with a badge and a gun whom nobody ever got to know. It was a picture of pride and loneliness Dan never forgot. Dan lived long enough under his father's watchful judgment to see and be on guard against his father's underlying rage that periodically exploded from the calm facade.

Fathers as a Group

Dan's story about his father is a lot like my story about my own father. It is also very similar to the stories of many of the men I have interviewed and counseled over the past eighteen years. Because we never got to know our fathers very well, we carry within us a kernel of the past that we have never understood, a piece of family history that keeps repeating itself with our wives, our children, and our friends. Dan's story is also the story of many fathers in the nineties who are trying to relate to their present families differently—sometimes "getting it right" but often missing the mark. These fathers have discovered that simply trying harder doesn't necessarily move them from the emotional outside into the hub of family life.

There are many cultural and personal reasons for this era of diminished fatherhood in which we are all living. In some ways, we are the victims of economic forces that came into play with the Industrial Revolution more than two hundred years ago. At that time, fathers left their farms and their cottage industries to work in factories far away from their families. The absentee father quickly became the second parent—the primary responsibility of child-rearing passed to mothers. Becoming the absent "breadwinner" had an emotional price tag attached to it for which we are still paying. It has been said that the love unit most damaged by the Industrial Revolution is the father-son relationship.

Looking at our Fathers and Ourselves

When I began interviewing fathers about their relationships with their own fathers, I tried to speak with men from different backgrounds in order to see if they had similar experiences as boys growing up in families. Most of the men I interviewed had never been asked by another man how they felt about their family histories and relationships. They were grateful for the opportunity to talk about themselves. I asked specific questions about what went on between their fathers and themselves. Some of the questions I asked were:

Were there any special activities that involved only your father and yourself?

Did your father ever take you aside and offer you his advice or his guidance?

Did your father ever teach you any of his skills?

What did your father tell you by his words or actions about what it meant to be a man? What did he "tell" you about what it meant to be in a relationship with a woman?

How did your father let people know his feelings, needs, and wants?

The answers that I heard had many similarities from one man to the next. "Father was almost never home." "When he was home, he didn't say much." "I wish he had spoken to me, given me guidance, told me that he loved me, that he approved of me."

By the time the interview was over, every man I spoke to seemed sad, and I felt their sadness too. When I extended my interviews to include men from different social groups and class backgrounds, the answers remained the same:

"Father was very quiet and reserved. I never knew what he was thinking or feeling."

"Father would get very mad and beat us, but we never really knew what wrong we had done to bring on such rage."

African-American men, Latinos and Anglo-Saxons, middle class and poor, college age and elderly, gay and straight men, all had very similar answers to the questions I posed. They had grown up in different families, but they all seemed to have the same father: a man who was remote, uncommunicative, and never available in a way that would have made a difference to his son. Though the life experiences of the men I interviewed were very different from one another, as sons they shared a common bond.

The Father Mystique

After I completed my interviews with men about their relationships with their fathers, I read extensively in the literature which was available on fathers and sons. As I grew in knowledge, I began to give workshops on fatherhood. I would start my lectures by directing the following question to the audience:

When I say the word 'father,' what's the first thing that comes to mind?

The groups that attended these workshops varied from young adults to the elderly, but the answers were usually the same:

"Father means protection."

"Father stands for strength."

"Father stands for rule of law."

"Father means to be provided for."

"Father means reason and logic."

The next question I asked was:

What was your dad really like?

There was always a pause. Then, stories began to flow from the group:

"Dad was rarely there. I hardly knew him."

"I wanted him to protect me, but he seemed to be hiding behind the newspaper."

"He was strict with me, but he never followed his own rules."

"He let my mother be in charge of everything."

"When my mother and he divorced, I almost never saw him again."

The gap between the ideal image of father and the real fathers that people in my workshops grew up with was enormous. However, I learned from this experience that a "father mystique"— a fantasy image of the ideal father—resides within many of us. This survives the emotional void in which most men seem to have been raised.

Father Loss

For many, the word "father" is synonymous with loss. Through abandonment, illegitimacy, divorce, and early death from poor health, alcohol, or overwork, losing fathers in many societies has become "normal." It has been estimated that more than half of our nation's children will spend at least some of their childhood growing up without a father in the home. As a society, we have come to expect the loss of fathers. Our low expectations of men as parents probably contribute to their flight from responsibility and involvement.

At a conference on men's roles in Washington, D.C., the leader of one workshop presented a videotape of his counseling sessions with a family under treatment. He was trying to illustrate how family therapy can help a marginally involved father move toward a more central position in his family. The man's wife was dying. During treatment, the father made strides in dealing with the needs of his sick wife and his children. The experience helped the entire family deal with the wife's death when it occurred and turned the survivors into a more cohesive unit. As the forty other men and I watched the last segment of the videotape, we heard the father state that after his wife died, he handed over the care of his children to his wife's mother. He had *decided* to become a visiting father to his children, rather than a custodial father. Neither the workshop leader nor any of the men in attendance questioned the man's decision. It wasn't expected that the father on the video screen would accept his responsibilities as a parent. We had all honored his male prerogative to "opt out" of managing a household for his children. Would we have had so little reaction if a mother had decided to abdicate her primary role after the death of her husband? And how is it that no one considered the potentially negative emotional impact that giving up his children would have on the father himself?

Do we lose fathers in part because we live in a culture that expects so little of them, or have we come to expect so little of fathers because we see them as marginal figures who are easily lost?

In this book, I examine the impact of losing a father and how individuals have learned to cope with this experience. I also examine the impact on fathers of the losses they suffer when they miss the opportunity to parent their children following divorce, a loss which we as a society tend to minimize.

Perhaps the most traumatic loss of a father is his sudden death. There is no way to prepare a child for the wrenching upset he or she will have to endure. Such was the case of Jane Meyers Drew, whose father died when she was an infant and who took on the study of this type of loss in her book *"Where Were You when I Needed You, Dad?": The Impact of a Father's Early Death.*

Jane Meyers Drew is a clinical psychologist in Newport Beach, California. She does public speaking and conducts workshops titled "Healing the Father Wound." I attended one of her workshops and learned a great deal about the connection between father loss and the resulting scars children carry throughout their lives. Ms. Drew has examined in detail the impact of the death of her father from heart failure when she was only fourteen months old and how growing up fatherless affected all aspects of her life. Drew associates certain statements and disclosures by herself and others with the lack of fathering that she and they have experienced:

> "I seldom think of my father without feeling sad or angry."
> "I expect too much of myself—and probably of others as well."
> "I am confused about my role as a man."
> "I lack confidence in my femininity."
> "I'm afraid that the people I love will leave me."
> "I feel fear frequently. I've developed a 'safe' life in order to avoid taking risks."
> "I have a difficult time breaking away from my mother's influence to become my own person."
> "I lack discipline and direction in my life."
> "When I'm close to success, something seems to hold me back from it."
> "I can't seem to make intimate relationships work for me."
> "I wonder if I'll ever be satisfied with myself."

Ms. Drew traces these expressions of insecurity and self-doubt to the "father wound." She divides her own father loss story into three acts.

The first lasted fourteen months in which she described her family as a normal one consisting of a mother, father, three older sisters, and an older brother. Her dad owned a filling station and garage, and her mother raised the children, gave piano lessons, and was the church organist.

Her father had childhood rheumatic fever, which gave him adult heart problems. Two weeks after his doctors sent him to a hospital he died of heart failure at age thirty-seven.

Drew writes, "Today, I understand that losing him was the most significant event in my life."

In act two she writes of her life from age fourteen to her thirties. As she was growing up her mother's dominating influence was paramount. All through school she missed having a father's attention and sought it by having wild crushes on boys.

In her early twenties she was depressed and had suicidal feelings and impulses. She either withdrew from men or chose those who were unable to reciprocate her feelings.

Ms. Drew describes the persistent self-doubts that plagued her as she pursued her career in psychotherapy. She has come to understand that she was continuing to search for a father by marrying a man twelve years her senior. In "Act Three" she is able to relate her chronic anguish and confusion to the loss of her husband and make sense out of her feelings of anger and grief. This enables her to examine the impact of this loss on her life.

She says:

> Reviewing how father loss had affected my adult life, I realized I didn't feel valuable unless I had a man to love me. I was uncomfortable in social situations because of harsh self-judgments. Much of the time I felt guilty and ashamed. Though driven to achieve and gain recognition, I often questioned my career choice and wondered about my life's purpose.

We do not simply "get over" the loss of a father, no matter how that loss has come about. The missing father has a residual impact on an individual throughout the life cycle. And, the less an individual is aware of the effect of the missing father, the more problems the person will face in his own parenting as well as other relationships.

2

CARRYING OUR FATHERS' FEELINGS

WE ARE ALL UNIQUE, as different as our thumb prints. As a teenager, I felt it was important to prove that I was different from my parents' generation, and I did that by the way I dressed and by the music to which I listened and danced. As an adult, I have continued to change and move in directions that my parents would never have considered for themselves.

Because of my attempts to be different, it is difficult for me to face the part of me that is similar to my parents, from whom I have tried so hard to distance myself. Yet there are ways in which I am just like the father I promised myself I would never become. I had always believed that my commitment to being a different kind of man than my father was based on my willpower and my ability to adopt new behaviors. I have since learned that the way I can stop repeating the past is by getting closer to it and gathering information about how our family behavior originated. This is the only way I have found to free me from carrying the feelings and behaviors I learned from my father into the life I am living today.

What's Your Dad Like?

Terry Kellogg, a leader in the Alcohol Recovery Movement, did a workshop in Aspen, Colorado. In it he decided to try an experiment with his audience to prove what a powerful impact fathers have on their adult children's lives. During several breaks in the lecture, participants were invited to come up to the podium and ask Terry individual questions. Whenever a personal problem was posed to him, Terry asked that person this question:

"What's your dad like?"

The first man said that he was having problems with anger and impatience. He told Terry that, no matter how hard he tried to get rid of his anger, he couldn't seem to change. Terry responded, "What was your dad like?"

"My dad?" the man said. "Oh. He was a pretty angry, impatient kind of guy."

"Have you dealt with that?" Terry asked.

"Oh, yeah. I worked really hard on things that have to do with Dad."

"But," Terry went on, "have you looked at the fact that you are living out your dad's life in the way you see other people, yourself, and your alcohol recovery process? In other words, the system you see things through is your dad's, and it's a way of keeping Dad alive by keeping his way of being alive in the world."

The second person who approached Terry had problems with boredom, depression, and feelings of hopelessness. When Terry asked, "What's your dad like?" the man answered, "My dad? He was a depressed man most of the time. He was kind of bored with life. He never inspired much hope." The same pattern of answers continued as a third and fourth person asked about himself. All the men discovered that they were, in fact, having the same problems in their lives as their fathers had experienced a generation earlier.

How do our fathers create such impacts on our lives? Mothers gave far more guidance in our day-to-day activities, and yet our fathers—the more silent and less present parent—seemed to exert a tremendous impact on how we continue to think and feel. When I look back at my own childhood, it appears strange to me that I appropriated so much of my father's way of being and behaving. He wasn't even that involved with me. He worked a lot during the "busy seasons." He read the newspaper in the evenings and later dozed off in front of the television set. After the age of fourteen, my father and I practically stopped talking to each other. Yet, in many important ways, I turned out to be like him.

About seven years ago, I was painting the benches on the porch of our newly purchased suburban home. My daughter Julie was seven at the time, and my younger daughter Hannah was barely five. Each had a paintbrush in hand. Hannah accidentally spilled some paint on the tarp while Julie was painting an area of the bench that I had already completed. At that moment, a surge of anger ran through me which I couldn't control. I snapped at Hannah for being "careless." Immediately, she began crying. Big tears rolled down her cheeks. Then I grabbed the paintbrush from Julie's tiny hand. They both retreated into the house, leaving me alone with the brushes, the half-filled paint cans, and spills. What had begun as an afternoon of fun with dad turned into a scene of fear and pain.

I was furious with myself for becoming so angry with my children. I had frightened them and made myself the object of their fear. But I was most disturbed by how easily I slipped into anger. My own father had done the same thing to me. It was a scene I had promised myself I would never repeat with my children. My father could be warm and gentle with an engaging sense of humor one minute, and the next minute turn stormy.

I can recall how much fun it was to sit on his knee at the window in our tiny Brooklyn apartment overlooking Lafayette Avenue and pick out the cars driving by that we wanted to own.

That was my father at his best: playful and sensitive. At his worst he was a rage-a-holic, a bully who could terrorize the entire household with a fury that began to build over days because of some minor incident or perceived slight. Then there were times when he became intensely jealous of my mother and imagined that she was seeing other men. When my father's anger eventually subsided, he became a kinder man, although he was capable of withdrawing into himself in a way that left me feeling lonely and unprotected. The paintbrush incident made me realize that what my dad had done to his children with his booming voice and threatening gestures I was also capable of doing to my children with an icy stare and an unkind word. My emotional response depressed me.

Too Much Therapy: Not Enough Change

Therapists are often said to be people in search of answers to their own problems. I guess I am no exception. I knew well before I had children that there were aspects of my personality which made me hard to live with, and I sought therapy to work on these issues over many years. But the area that changed the least after all this therapy was my unwarranted anger. Anger continued to take its toll on my life, despite my best efforts to control it.

I went through years of "insight-oriented" psychotherapy. The therapist examined what had happened to me as a child, my impressions of who my parents were, and what they had done to me as I was growing up. He tried to get me to connect my anger to the love I believed I had not gotten as a child. When that didn't produce the results I was seeking, I moved on to a behaviorist who used what he termed "rational-emotive" techniques. The behaviorist focused on my thinking and the ways that I might control my anger by anticipating the triggers that would set me off in the present. He wasn't interested in what occurred in my past.

I cannot say I gained nothing from my years of conventional psychotherapy. It certainly helped me develop the skills that allow me to do the counseling work I do today. But, it seems to me, much of what passes for therapy is highly overrated as a means toward changing our behaviors. The behaviorist who narrowly focused on my thought patterns ignored the human dimension of my family history over many years and generations. The therapist who offered insight was more empathetic, but he seemed to accept my memories of the relationship my parents and I had as some kind of emotional "fact." He suggested that my anger disguised my grief over what my parents had done to me or not given to me. But I never "got in touch" with that grief in his office, and he never challenged my notions about who my parents really were or are today.

No therapist ever advised me to speak to my father, or my mother, or my sister, all of whom I had lost contact with by the time I was twenty-one. And that was exactly what I needed to do. When I finally did reconnect with them, I came to understand who I was and how I got that way. In looking back, I can see that much of the therapy I received merely recycled my childhood view of reality. It never helped me to grow up and gain a realistic view of the past, nor did it advise me to go home again to find the source and solution to my current anger problems.

Therapy's Best Kept "Secret"

One family therapist who had a different way of looking at the process by which people change was Murray Bowen. He did most of his research between 1954 and 1974. Although he was trained as a psychiatrist, he was able to focus away from the inner workings of the mind and onto the emotional connections between family members. Bowen stopped putting the blame on mothers and fathers for the emotional disturbances of their adult children. Instead, he saw the family as a system of emotional relationships that is passed almost intact from generation to generation. This system plays a crucial role in the formation of the adult person we become. Bowen developed a complicated theory about change that breaks down into this formula:

An individual may be able to achieve the most important growth in his behavior and his relationships if he remains calm and clearheaded enough to reconnect as an adult with the most important people from his childhood. Bowen discovered that if we are able to return to our fathers, mothers, sisters, and brothers without trying to get them to change—but simply with a willingness to learn more about who they are and are not, then, and over time—we will be able to make strides in all of our endeavors and relationships.

Returning Home to Speak to Your Father, Your Mother, and Your Significant Others

I knew that I was emotionally cut off from the important people in my childhood. As a therapist, I knew work had to be done with my family. What was stopping me from doing it? I felt that I had spent so many years of my life trying to get away from my family and trying to be different from them that I was scared to get involved with them again. I was afraid I would lose the independence that I had worked so hard to achieve.

I remember watching the miniseries *Roots* at about this time and thinking that I would like to know more about the history of my family. But Bowen was asking us to do more than simply find out about births, deaths, marriages, and other facts that might be learned from our family trees. He was suggesting that we would benefit by going back and speaking to our fathers in ways in which we might not be accustomed. He didn't mean the "Hi, Dad. Bye, Dad" that occurs at family gatherings. He meant we should find out about our father's life before he married our mother and decided to have his own family. The idea was to begin learning something new about what was happening to our father's family when *he* was growing up.

This might begin with me saying, "Dad, I once heard you say that your mother and father fought a lot. Can you remember what caused their fights? What else was going on in your family at the time?"

Part of us may think, "What possible value can there be in finding out what went on more than fifty years ago in my father's family?" However, if our fathers are able and willing to speak with us, we may discover that their experiences with family conflicts were quite similar to the ones we witnessed as children, and that those fights may have a striking resemblance to the way we handle disagreements and differences with our own wives and families. History has a tendency to repeat itself in families, and although the players change over the generations, the patterns of behavior remain very much the same. As my father's son, I have discovered that despite all my insights and desire to change, I have remained loyal to his ways of thinking and doing things. I find myself saying and doing some of the things to my own children that he said and did to me.

The process of helping a person to understand the connection between his present problems and the family in which he grew up and continues to be a member is called "coaching." This is a word usually associated with sports and is a concept most men readily understand. Murray Bowen first used the word to describe the changing role of therapists who had begun to look at families in a new way. To many people, seeing a therapist means that something is very wrong. Seeing a "coach" implies something different. We all need help with our lives from time to time. We can all use some coaching. In the next chapter, I will show how this concept can be a valuable approach to improving the quality of men's lives.

3

COACHING

coach *n.* One who instructs the players in the fundamentals of a
competitive sport and directs team strategy. *v.* To train intensively
(as by instruction and demonstration).

Merriam Webster's Collegiate Dictionary
Tenth Edition

The Importance of Coaching in Men's Lives

FROM LITTLE LEAGUE BASEBALL DIAMONDS to professional
basketball courts, the coach is a symbol of positive male
authority. For the great majority of American boys who have
received so little guidance from men, the athletic coach has been
the father figure whose approval we sought. Those of us lucky
enough to have played under a good coach were taught skills by a
man who was willing to communicate his knowledge of the game.
Pre-game motivational meetings and "locker room chats" were as
close as most of us would ever get to a spiritual experience.

Unfortunately, for many men like me who grew up in
schoolyards and athletic fields, whatever coaching and male

camaraderie we experienced ended in high school or perhaps college. We now sit in offices and corporate board rooms or we stand on the shop floor facing machines. As I watch effective coaches in action, I realize there is much that I can learn from them about working with men. Once, I observed Lenny Wilkins during an Atlanta Hawks game. He was pacing the sidelines, very alert to all that was going on around him. As a coach, Wilkins knows his players very well, and he knows the strategies that work best with the men on his team.

During the Atlanta Hawks game, the action on the field was important to him, but he also needed to have an idea of the group dynamics among his players. A good coach knows the limitations of his role. He gets to direct strategy from the sidelines, but he is aware that he is not a player in the game itself. The team members ultimately get to decide what is going to happen on the playing field.

I have observed poor coaches who seem to have many problems in common. If you've ever gotten involved in organized children's sports, you have probably seen a coach who is out of touch with his role and is overly invested in his own ego. This kind of coach is so focused on winning that he has lost sight of the children in front of him. The team members are irritable with each other, and they no longer focus on strategy and form. They are preoccupied with the mood of the coach, and they are too busy watching the veins in his neck to engage in a high level of play. This coach has stepped from the sidelines onto the playing field, and the players have lost control of the action.

A successful coach wants to have a constant flow of information so that he can use what he learns to create new strategies to improve the level of play. He needs to keep in mind the larger picture of the team working together while not losing sight of the individuals involved and his role.

Therapist as Coach

Successful athletic coaching and effective therapy have much in common. When therapy does what it is meant to do, the therapist, like the athletic coach, stands on the sidelines. He offers his client knowledge and some strategies for managing life's problems and key relationships. What is wrong with most traditional psychotherapy is that the therapist often makes himself too important in the change process. Many people who come for help are encouraged to work on their problems *with* the therapist as if the problems are between *them*. If feelings from other important relationships get stirred up, it is also considered a good thing to explore those feelings with the *therapist*. You get to talk *about* your family, but it is considered less important that you speak to them. The person seeking help becomes very attached and dependent on the therapist, and his natural network of support and information—his family—is often ignored. I have found that men, even more than most women, need the type of coaching that will encourage them to reconnect with their first families and also teach them the skills needed to do this.

Coaching can be helpful in a couple of ways.

First, men generally are less effective in the use of "people skills" than women are. As a rule, and with notable exceptions, men have not been as well trained as women in the art of intimate conversation and the awareness of other people's needs. Coaching performs remedial work in this important area.

Second, because of the man's role as the "breadwinner" and as the "instrumental one" in the family over many generations, men have come to occupy an *outsider* position. Our wives become the "social planners" who are in charge of all relationships, and as a result, we often have little direct communication with friends and relatives, and even our own children. Distance and cutoffs from our own fathers and mothers place a tremendous unseen burden on our marriages. Coaching for reconnection with our relatives is the key to having marriages that are not over-loaded with unresolved issues from our first families.

By the time a man comes to see me, he usually has exhausted all of his efforts to solve things on his own, and his problem has often reached crisis proportions. Succumbing to the myth of male invincibility, he often thinks that he should have been able to "fix things" by himself. He views coming to see me as an admission of failure. If a man is exploding with anger at home, he might want me to offer a quick technique to help him control the explosions. Many men are quite happy once they are relieved of the symptom that was disturbing them. They do not want to look at other issues in their lives that may be connected to the problem. As a coach, I try to expand the scope of a man's work once his initial problem has calmed down. I would like to see the father in front of me get in touch with his own father and mother to learn more about who he is and how he got that way. It is this type of family work that will make the most profound change in his life.

An example of the work I try to do can be seen in the following dialogue between myself and a father who has just made some important changes in a marriage that was on the verge of falling apart. John had been "blocking out" his wife and his children for years until finally his wife, Susan, began threatening him with divorce. At the time of this dialogue John was feeling pretty good because things had "settled down" between Susan and himself. He began talking about ending his work with me. But I knew more coaching had to be done if John and Susan were to maintain a good marriage and if John were to become an effective, loving parent. I encouraged John to do some more work with his own father whom John had little to do with over the years. I tried to coach him into a new position in his first family which would consolidate the gains he has made in his marriage.

COACH: You did some nice work with Susan this past week. It sounds like you were able to listen to what she had to say, and you also got to say what you needed without an explosion. The children, Alan and Sheryl, sound like they are calmer too, since they know you two are not about to split up.

JOHN: Yeah. Well, I almost lost it at one point, but I concentrated on what you told me about biting my tongue to make sure I don't cut off what Susan has to say, even though I feel she's dead wrong some of the time.

COACH: I don't know if you remember, but I asked you during our first meeting if you could tell me where you learned how to block Susan out the way you do. You said you weren't sure where you picked that up, and that as far as you could remember, you had always been that way. I'd like to ask you that question again. Where do you think you learned to block out other people's ideas they way you sometimes do?

JOHN: (Long pause.) I can hardly remember when that began, because it's been going on for so long. It feels like I just always did that to her and she never liked it. It feels like we fought about it from day one.

COACH: Then let me put it another way. Is there anyone else in your life, past or present, who could also block people out and not listen to them?

JOHN: My dad was not much for listening to anyone. He was kind of a loner. We all knew that you didn't go to Dad unless you had to . . . sort of like me in a way.

COACH: Was your dad like that with your mother, too?

JOHN: I guess he was. Dad could block out anyone. Come to think of it, I can remember them fighting about the same thing. Mom would complain that what she said didn't count and he would just shut up and get real quiet. If she pressed him, he would explode. We all knew to stand back from him.

COACH: Have you ever thought about what made it so hard for your dad to listen to your mom or you?

JOHN: No, I guess I never did. I just always figured that was the way Dad was. I never gave it much thought.

COACH: Where is your dad living now?

JOHN: Dad lives by himself now, outside of Paterson. He and Mom divorced about seven years ago after my sister Kathy moved out. I don't speak to him much.

COACH: When was the last time you spoke to him?

JOHN: (After a long pause.) About six months ago around Thanksgiving. Dad retired last year. He plays a lot of golf now. He has this group of golf buddies he hangs out with. Then he goes to the club for drinks. He's doing all right these days, I guess.

COACH: What was it like when you saw Dad last?

JOHN: It was like it always was. Dad didn't say much. We shot nine holes together. He was okay.

COACH: It sounds like you and he still don't say much to each other.

JOHN: Nah. Dad hasn't changed much over the years. He's still real quiet and to himself.

COACH: Actually, I see you and your dad as having a lot in common. You both have had a hard time listening to your wives and your kids. And you have both gotten into major conflicts with your wives over this. You both get really angry when you feel that people are putting pressure on you to change.

JOHN: Yeah. Well, I guess some of that is true. I never

thought about me and Dad being that alike. I always tried to be different from the way he was.

COACH: Have you ever considered finding out more about how your dad got to be such a loner, how come he has such a hard time when people try to get him to listen to them?

JOHN: I know Dad doesn't like to talk about stuff like that. The only thing we ever get into is either golf or his job. Now, he isn't even working.

COACH: If I were to tell you that it would go a long way toward helping you figure out your own problems with your wife and kids if you were able to gather some more information about how your dad got to be the man he is, would you consider asking him a few questions when you feel the time is right?

JOHN: I'll think about it. But, like I said, Dad doesn't speak much. But I guess I don't ask him much either.

COACH: Why don't you just think about what it would be like for you to approach your dad . . . just to think about how you might ask him some questions about his own life if you decided to do that.

John decided to continue working with me although he was highly skeptical about his efforts to get his father to speak about anything more than his golf score. It took him six weeks to arrive at the point where he felt ready to approach his father with a few questions about his father's life before he had children. In the three meetings John and I had during this time he expressed his uneasiness about this "assignment." John said, "I don't think this is going to work."

And I responded, "Would you be willing to try?"

John began to realize that it was no longer just his father's resistance to change that he was dealing with, but his own. John tried to imagine how he might introduce the topic to his father. Then he came in for the next session saying that he hadn't gotten to do it that week. John and I figured out together that asking his father any question was breaking a family rule with which John had grown up.

It was the rule called: "Don't Do Anything That Might Upset Your Father—Or Else!"

Finally, John found the right time to ask his father the questions he had rehearsed. His father did not explode as John feared. He answered his son's initial questions and then offered a description of his childhood. He spoke about a family life in which rules were so rigidly enforced that army boot camp seemed mild by comparison. The "rule of silence" was the law of the household, and "opening your mouth" to your father in any way was met by the threat of violence. John felt his father's underlying sadness when his father said that he had tried to have a different relationship with his own children and then admitted he had always felt like a failure in this area.

John went through a mild depression after his father opened up to him about his disappointments and regrets. I worked with John around the idea that the sadness that he was finally experiencing was a grief that had been carried by the men in his family and passed on from father to son. It was probably several generations old. John began speaking with other members of his extended family, including cousins, uncles and aunts whom he hadn't seen in years. He discovered that the "rule of silence" and the pattern of "blocking people out" were not unique to his grandfather, his father, and himself. It was part of a larger family pattern that seemed to exist throughout his family in different ways.

I consider the work that John did with his father and his extended family to be the most significant emotional work that a person can do. During his early sessions with me, John learned stopgap techniques with which to control his self-destructive behavior in his marriage. If he had stopped at that point, I do not believe the tools that he acquired would have been sufficient to save his marriage and his family.

The work that John did with his father helped him to create a different sense of himself. John was able to use what he learned in this reunion to create a better relationship with his children and his wife. He could no longer block out members of his family without bringing the painful story of his father's childhood into awareness. This dialogue between John and me from a more recent session brings into sharper focus the changes that he made:

COACH: So what has it been like these days when you spend time alone with Alan and Sheryl?

JOHN: Sometimes I feel a little blue when I'm with them but I don't get angry like I used to, and I don't believe that I've been blocking them out. I do have my dad in my head a lot now, and I still think about how much I turned out like him. I don't know whether thinking about him so much after all these years is good or bad . . . maybe a little sad in the way you and I spoke about before.

COACH: I'd like to say that you've made some important changes in the way that you once kept people at a distance. It's probably a good idea for you to continue spending time with your kids and thinking about your connection to your father even though you're feeling blue. How are Sheryl and Alan reacting to you now?

JOHN: Alan said that I was being very "quiet" the other day, and Sheryl has been asking to do things with me. I don't think either of them have said that they wanted to do something with me in years. I would just like to get over this feeling of being down.

John was feeling depressed at this point in his work, but he was able to let go of his most self-destructive behavior. He was also able to experience the grief that men in his family have been avoiding for generations, and he has developed an adult position in his extended family. He was taking greater responsibility for all of his relationships, and has become "more of a self" in every aspect of his life.

Can Men Really Handle This Kind of Work?

Because of effective utilization of the coaching technique, John was able to reconnect with an extremely difficult father and establish a new relationship with his entire family. I have done significant work within my own extended family that involved breaking longstanding family rules. I had to learn to stay on task in the face of family pressure to return to the old nonuseful patterns of behavior I once employed. John and I have much in common. We both grew up in a male "culture" that has given us rigid guidelines on what it means to be a man and the acceptable ways that men behave. We were taught to be strong, work hard, and compete always. We were also brought up with the idea that relationships and the emotional issues occurring between people are women's work and that our job as men is to stay focused on more concrete tasks. Even now I sometimes find myself becoming so involved in fixing something or in reaching a goal that I may lose sight of what is going on between myself and the people I care about. As men, we pay a large price for our lack of awareness of the emotional needs of others.

On the other hand, much of the male culture that I have been describing has been analyzed and criticized by women and not men. Our training in being the "strong and silent" sex has militated against our producing spokesmen who might present life from our point of view. The women's movement has gone a long way toward producing equality for women and toward encouraging men to participate in the lives of children. However, we men must also develop our own voice to describe our unique experience.

As men and as fathers, we should examine our limitations, without disregarding our strengths. I have come to believe that some aspects of what might be called "traditional" male culture, with its emphasis on tasks and logic, can play an important role in the self-help work that I am advocating. When I consider the work that I have done within my family, I also give credit to aspects of the training I received about what it means to be a man. I've listed some of these effective qualities that relate to gender:

- Courage is an important part of being a man, but I had to broaden my view of bravery from dealing only with physical dangers to include areas requiring emotional integrity and strength.
- A man has to work hard for whatever he gets and sometimes he has to roll up his sleeves and get his hands dirty.
- Persistence and even aggressiveness at times is important, as is the ability not to give up in the face of resistance.
- Logic, strategy, and well-thought-out tactics should be used when approaching a situation. In my case some of this philosophy comes from my participation in team sports.
- Remain cool under fire and don't lose the capacity to think clearly in tense situations.
- Stay on task in the face of emotions that might cause a loss of balance and lead to disorganized thinking.

These are qualities that I feel are needed to be successful in doing some of the work that I outline in the coming chapters. As men, we suffer more from an unwillingness to do the type of family work that I illustrate than from any other limitations.

THE NATURE
OF THE WORK

To CHANGE BEHAVIORS THAT have not worked, men need to go back to their family of origin—this is the most challenging environment in which you can work. As has been said by one popular family therapist and author, "If we can move toward gathering a more factual history of our family . . . and if we can learn to be more objective in our own family, other relationships will be a piece of cake."

There is no simple formula on how to reconnect with your first family, but there is some basic knowledge that anyone who attempts it should possess.

Do I Need to Have a Coach?

You may wish to work with a coach, or you might see this as a self-help project that you would like to try on your own. I would advise men who are accustomed to working alone to try working with a coach on a project like this that involves both thinking and feeling. One of the advantages of working with a coach has to do with the intensity of the feelings that inevitably get stirred up when we try to change family patterns of behavior. As easy as it may be for us to remain calm and objective in less personal situations, it is virtually impossible to stay objective when we try to reconnect with important people from our past. This happens because our emotional attachments to our parents and siblings are never fully resolved. A coach is able to challenge our reactions and not take sides, either for us or for our parents, and he can also help us to get back on track when we wander off. Your coach may be a professional therapist who is trained to do family of origin work. Your coach can also be a men's group or even a friend who has basic understanding of family dynamics and is willing to take the time to understand the ground rules that I am about to enumerate. You may also begin this work on your own if you have some rudimentary knowledge about how family systems operate and are willing to get help if you get stuck. People you should not ask to take on the role of coach are wives or anyone else who is emotionally involved with either you or your family.

Look for these specific qualities of a good coach in the person you select:

1) A coach must be someone who is able to remain objective when discussing emotionally charged situations.

2) A coach must be able to remain neutral and not "take sides" when family issues are presented to him. He should be able to focus on what the pattern is *between* people rather than who is "right" or "wrong."

3) A coach should be someone who is naturally curious. He needs to be able to continually generate questions about family members to the person he is coaching and never believe that "the final truth" has been reached.

4) A coach should be a person who is able to make suggestions and then step back. He should not be someone who is so controlling that he has to take over.

5) A coach needs to have patience. He needs to encourage the person he is coaching to work at his own pace.

6) A coach should be able to think strategically and anticipate what might happen next in a situation.

7) A coach should be an individual who has achieved a high level of maturity and independence within his own family of origin. (This is called achieving a high level of "differentiation" in the model that I present.)

Before You Begin: A Few Cautionary Notes

1. This Is Not a Quick-Fix Approach to Change

Even though this model is in a self-help format, whatever you accomplish will not occur in three easy steps. You will need to proceed slowly and thoughtfully or you will stir up more anxiety than you or your family can handle. If you work at a reasonable pace that acknowledges the generations it took to create the unique blend of strengths and problems that is your family, then you will be less inclined to try to complete your work quickly.

2. You Cannot Lose or Fail in Doing This Work

It is *predictable* that when you attempt to approach your mother, father, or some other significant person from your first family in a new way, they will react in the old way. You may even find yourself repeating the same family fight that you had when you were twelve years old. *This is not something that is wrong.* This happens because *all* systems resist change of any kind. If you lose your objectivity and get caught in the old patterns, it does not mean that you have failed. It is time to go back either to the drawing board or your coach.

3. Stay Focused on the Personal Benefits of This Work

If you keep in mind that you are returning home to speak with important people from your past for *you* and *not for your family*, you will be less likely to act out or drop out when things don't go the way you expected. *You are not trying to get your mother or father to change who they are.* You will change in the way that you manage your relationship with your wife, children, in-laws, and even your boss if you are able to stay focused on your tasks in the face of other people's resistance.

So, tell me again. What's the purpose of speaking to my mother and father, and what am I supposed to do with this new information that I am trying to gather?

As we grow up in our families, we eventually develop fixed ideas about who our parents are. Most of our views about our parents were formed when we were children. Children are great at observing what is going on around them, but they usually come up with a distorted view when they try to understand the meaning of events and their own part in them. Sometimes children blame themselves for events like divorces and deaths that have nothing to do with them. They can also blame their mothers and fathers for what they feel their parents did or did not do for them. The problem with our childhood interpretations is that they are sometimes thirty or forty years behind the times. Our early views about our parents have never been updated, and we are frozen with them in the past.

The way in which we see ourselves in the present has very much to do with how we see our mothers and fathers. The stories that we tell about the families we grew up in tend to justify to ourselves what we have become. The labeling of parents as "toxic," and families as "dysfunctional," prevents us from taking the steps that would allow us to grow up.

Who hasn't said something like this at one time or another: "I know I don't give a lot of praise to anyone, but when I was growing up, no one ever gave me compliments or encouragement either."

We base our present selves on how we see the central figures from our past. *But what if our view of those very important people was to change?* Most therapists remain faithful to the idea that you're stuck with your "introjects"—those people that we take in as children and around whom our personalities are formed. I have not found that to be so. I have seen significant changes in people who work with their families of origin as adults. In this type of work, we return to the original figures from our childhood whom we may believe have hurt us or not given us what we needed in order to mature.

We neither confront them with what we feel we never received, nor do we look to give them a hug and forgive them for what they did. We just return with an open mind and a spirit of curiosity to try to learn more about who they were before and who they are now.

Here is an example of the change process in this type of family work:

1) I begin to ask my father some well-thought-out questions about his family life when he was growing up and his experience of being a father and a husband when I was growing up. I learn many things about him that I never knew before.

2) As I gather this new information about my father's life, I also gain new perspectives on how he came to be the man he is today and the father he was to me when I was a child. I find myself less inclined to blame him, and *I find myself moving away from the central position of the hurt child who never had his needs met.*

3) As my view of my father changes and my relationship with him shifts, *my view of myself changes.* I have reached what Bowen would call a "higher level of differentiation."

Dealing with Our Own Resistance

We may benefit from the changes that we make, but most of us resist them every step of the way. Our fathers and mothers may resist the questions that we begin to ask about their lives or the new ways in which we approach them. We, in turn, may avoid finding out too much, or breaking an unwritten family rule such as, "Don't poke around where you don't belong." We are part of a family emotional system, and we respond to its rules. If the family messages that come back to us when we try something new or different are "Tread lightly," or even, "You've just stepped over the line with that question," then these messages will stir up anxiety for us as well as for them. Trying to speak to your father alone but always getting "referred" to your mother instead is a typical example of a family's resistance to change.

What if My Father or Mother Was Abusive, Violent, or Extremely Rejecting to Me as a Child?

It may seem self-destructive to return to what feels like "the scene of the crime," or "the home of the criminal," but that is exactly what adults who have been violated or neglected as children will benefit from doing. It may take a great deal of preparation and a dedicated coach, but reconnecting, as an adult, with an abusive father or mother is an extremely empowering act. Children are powerless and at the mercy of their parents. Adults are able to return and use their adult powers of observation to learn something about the man or woman who caused them so much pain as children. The decision to step back and observe is a significant new position to take. It is also a position that we could never have taken as a child. The impulse to back away or drop out from this task is a potent one. Some of the reasons people give to not do this kind of work are:

1) Why should I go back and speak to my father? I know exactly how he'll respond. He always reacts the same way!

2) My father's done so much to me that I'll never be able to speak to him about anything more than the weather. The damage has already been done, as far as I'm concerned.

3) Why should I open myself up to him? I'll just get the same old stuff dumped back on me.

4) I've spent most of my life trying to get away from my father and what happened to me in his house. There's no way I'm going to have anything to do with him.

5) I already know how he got to be the way he is. There's really not a whole lot for me to find out.

6) He's never going to change, so what's the use?

7) Things aren't too bad between me and my father now. I don't want to stir things up and create a problem.

8) I've always had a good relationship with my father and mother. There's no reason for me to ask questions or to bring up anything new.

Anyone considering returning home to reconnect with parents may have already had one or more of the reactions that I have listed. It's a safe bet that more of these reactions will be experienced as an individual does more of this type of work with his or her family.

Every one of the reactions listed above is focused on mother and father and getting them to change. When we do this kind of work, the focus must always remain on ourselves and our own reactions to what is going on between ourselves and others.

5

WHERE AND
HOW TO BEGIN

A MAN WHO DECIDES to use his family of origin as a vehicle for change should begin with a problem that he is now having. The problem may come in the form of a complaint from his wife or children. His children may say, "Daddy, you never play with us anymore. You promise, but then you always get busy with something else." And your wife might add, "And when you're with the family, it never seems like you're here. Your mind is always somewhere else."

Such criticisms are annoying to hear from your family when you know that you're working as hard as you can to provide for them, and you have a lot on your mind. You may begin to feel resentful and say to yourself, "Can't they just cut me a little slack? If I'm thinking about other things, it's because I've got a lot of responsibilities. I'm working to support them."

Though in the beginning such small conflicts are irritating but unimportant, they may turn into sticking points between yourself and your wife and children over time. You may start mumbling to yourself, "If she would just get off my back." At the same time your wife may be saying to herself, "If he would just be there for the kids and me when I ask him to."

When there is a problem between partners, it always feels like the other party needs to change in order for the climate to improve. No one ever comes into my office with a marital problem and says, "I have a problem that I need to change." The focus is always on the other person. However, real change begins with you.

We Don't Begin by Doing—We Begin by Thinking

First, we need to change the way we perceive. We have to be ready to imagine new and different possibilities. The husband who is being told by his wife that he is not making himself available to her or his children needs to be able to reflect on her statement and not just react to it. If he is only able to react to what he feels is criticism or lack of appreciation, then he and his wife will once again repeat a marital fight that they have experienced all too often.

The husband might say, "You never appreciate how hard I work. You just criticize me for not being available."

His wife might counter, "If you would just make yourself a little more available, I could show you the appreciation you deserve."

Such a couple is stuck in a destructive pattern that keeps repeating itself. As things heat up and tensions escalate, they will increasingly blame one another as the cause of the problem.

Each partner in this conflict is highly focused on what is happening *between them* in the present. But each would benefit greatly from taking a step back and examining the relationship *between this problem and the past.*

Unless we decide to do some research on our families of origin, we remain unaware that the patterns that we often play out in our marriages are tied to the emotional systems in which we grew up. The rules that we live by and the roles that we play are determined by what has already occurred in our family history. This will happen despite all our efforts to be different from our parents.

The husband who is being told that he is unavailable will gain little from continuing to battle with his wife. He *will* move forward if he returns to his first family and begins to study how his father and other male relatives participated in the lives of their families. He will grow infinitely more from asking his father or uncle or grandfather about the pressures on them than he will from blaming his wife for being too demanding. He may also need to realize that his wife may resent the traditional way that household tasks are being divided. She would also benefit from speaking to her mother, aunts, and other women in her family about how they handled their families and their feelings when their husbands were not available. If the husband and wife are able to learn more about how individuals in their first families managed their lives, they will have gained knowledge about themselves. They will bring a more developed sense of self back to their own marriage.

As a rule, those couples who are willing to work on relationships with members of their first families are better able to resolve problems in their marriages than are couples who receive marriage counseling that only focuses on problems between the partners. Sometimes, we are not going to solve problems with our wives until we've gathered information from our fathers or addressed important issues with our mothers.

Gathering information about our first families is not always easy. This is because families are emotional organizations in which strong feelings may be simmering below an apparently calm surface. I have been told by people whom I have coached that "Nothing much has gone on between myself and my parents for years." They were surprised to experience an emotional scene and a flood of negative feelings when they decided to initiate closer contact and new behaviors. This is why it is so important to develop strategies to implement the moves that you may decide to make.

If we approach our families in old familiar ways, then we are guaranteed to get the same responses we have gotten in the past. We will also confirm our feelings about our parents and other important people from our past. Most likely, we will come away with a statement like this: "I knew they'd never change! I don't even know why I bother to see them."

On the other hand, if I have only spoken about sports with my father, can I expect him to initiate a personal conversation with me just because I now feel that it would be good for that to occur? I may spend my entire life saying that my father is a man who only speaks about sports.

Families tend to repeat similar patterns over time. We participate with other members to maintain the status quo.

If we approach our parents with criticism, or in a confrontational manner, we will usually be met with defensiveness or withdrawal. The only approach to our first families that enhances our adulthood and promotes personal growth is a positive one that is carefully thought out. Trying to ask a parent a few informational questions may become an emotionally charged experience.

The ability to remain objective (but not detached) in the intense emotional environment of our first families indicates a high level of emotional maturity and is an important goal in this type of work.

Adopting the Research Stance

When I was a kid playing softball in the schoolyard, I fell into a batting slump. The coach suggested that my stance at the plate was not right and gave me techniques to correct it. Unlike softball, family of origin work requires only one stance to be effective, and that is known as the *research stance.*

The research stance is the position taken by the newspaper reporter and the laboratory scientist in getting information. Both may be very involved in their work, but they can only be effective as long as they retain their objectivity. It may seem strange to visit your parents using the criteria of scientific observation and academic study, but that is the only position that will allow you to gain the information needed to make the changes that you need in yourself. This is not to say that you should remain unemotional or detached: the goal is ultimately to be able to remain intimately involved but noncondemning and open with all of the important people in your life. In this way you will be able to evaluate the information you gain and handle your own response more effectively. You will be able to change and become your own person. The reason we need to remain objective about what is going on between ourselves and our parents is that the emotional field between us is often so intense that we are almost guaranteed to lose our powers of observation and repeat old negative patterns of behavior if we allow ourselves to become stuck in old patterns of response.

Recently, I was driving my wife and mother-in-law to an engagement when the topic turned to relatives neither had seen since my wife's late teenage years. I knew that my wife wanted to know more about what was going on at that time from her mother's perspective. She began to ask questions about her mother's life at a time when she herself had left home. At this time her mother began to live with an ex-husband whom my wife always disliked. My wife was so emotionally involved she could not maintain her objectivity as she opened up this very intense topic. She started out asking, neutrally, "What was going on with you at that time, Mom?" but as her emotions got involved her question became, "What was going on in your life that was so important that you couldn't see that I needed to come back and live at home?"

As my wife lost more of her research stance her mother also acutely reacted to what she experienced as her daughter's criticism. She defended herself and justified her own behavior, and the dialogue ended with each in a neutral corner. If my wife had maintained a more objective stance, she might have learned more about what was really going on with her mother at that time and why her mother made the decisions that she did. She would have gotten a more accurate picture of her mother's way of thinking and feeling, and how that might be similar to the thought processes of other members of her family and even herself.

We can all become reactive when we talk about a charged emotional topic with someone in our first family. We lose the research stance, and our capacity to gather new information is also temporarily lost.

Thinking about the System

I refer to families as "emotional systems" in this book. The word system is one way to describe how families perform the practical and emotional tasks they need to do. In order to reconnect successfully with your first family, it is important to understand how family systems work.

A factory operates as a system; so do our bodies and our cars. Any organization, organism, or machine in which people or parts interact forms some type of system. When we think about families as systems, it becomes less important to figure out the *causes* of problems and more important to examine *how the parts operate together*.

For example, you are watching a man walk his dog and observe the system that operates between them. Every time the dog pulls on the leash, the man hits the dog. And each time that the man hits his dog, the dog pulls harder on the leash. This pattern continues as man and dog struggle down the block. The next morning as you are going to work, you observe the man and his dog going through the same ritual as the day before.

The dog and his master have created a simple system between them. After a while, it becomes irrelevant who started all of this; it simply evolves into *the way this system operates*.

Looking at the world and many of the things within it as systems is a departure from the way most of us were trained to think. Before I learned about systems, I had always examined events from the perspective of cause and effect: event *B* occurred only because Event *A* had occurred first. But cause and effect cannot explain the complexity of many of the things that happen in our families and our lives.

Cause and effect thinking in a family situation might be indicated by the man who says, "On March fourteenth my wife began to shout at me. I hate being yelled at because of an incident that happened when I was a child. So, I packed my bags and decided to file for divorce."

Looking at the same incident from the perspective of the family as an emotional system, we might hear the man say, "Over the twelve years of our marriage, Helen and I have had problems managing conflict together. We each felt pressure from our parents to stay together, and our children have been acting up since we've spoken to them about our plans to separate. We worked with a marriage counselor for six months but things did not improve between us. On March fourteenth I decided to move in with a friend."

In some ways it may seem simpler to look for the cause of the family or marital problem in our spouse, or even in the way we were treated as children. There is a universal tendency to blame someone else when things become tense or don't go the way we would like. Blame is always what is called a *reactive* position. This means that you've temporarily lost your ability to think objectively about the real dynamics going on *between you* and the other person.

Family Connections

All the actions and events that go on among husbands, wives, and children in a family are part of the way the system operates. If one part of the system changes, impact will be felt somewhere else. If a parent loses his job, the reverberations will be felt by each family member. With less money available, one child might not be able to go to camp and another might have to stop his weekly music lessons. Father may decide that he can't afford to bowl on weekends, and the parents' night out plus baby-sitting expenses are too costly to remain a weekly treat. The parent who lost the job may feel depressed, but might also be more available for the children during the day. Tensions might rise in the marriage and one of the children may start misbehaving in school.

If you entertain doubts about whether your family actually operates as a system with highly interactive parts, try this experiment:

Change one behavior that you do on a daily basis and involves direct contact with family members. If you normally go into everybody's room to say good night, try not doing that for a week. If you are usually noncommunicative at the dinner table, tell everybody a lot about your day. Then observe how family members respond to your new behavior. Also see how you respond to their reactions.

Family members tend to minimize how connected each member is to every other member and that a change in any member of the system will have an impact on someone else.

Wars, recessions, births, deaths, marriage, and separations of all kinds will heighten anxiety and affect each member of the family in his or her own way. If the anxiety level exceeds the family's capacity to handle it, symptoms may appear in the marriage, one of the spouses, or one or more of the children. This is apparent to many of us as we participate in family life and experience the stress of daily events. What is less apparent and equally important is the way the nuclear family—the part of the family that includes the mother, father, and children—relates to the extended family, or what I have been describing as the family of origin.

The nuclear family is emotionally connected to the extended family in very important ways. Distance and cutoffs between these two interlocking systems can be dangerous to a family's emotional health.

The importance of parents' relationships with their own fathers and mothers becomes clearer when the vital connections between the parts of the extended family system are better understood. Intensity from one part of a system that is not being dealt with can easily invade another area of family relatedness without our knowledge of its source.

Dee and Harry, one couple I counseled, experienced the death of Harry's father while I was seeing them. Despite my encouragement to express their feelings, they said little about this significant loss, and no process of grieving seemed to be taking place. As I continued to work with this family over the course of that year, numerous symptoms appeared in members of the extended family that seemed removed from the original loss. Cousins and grandchildren had a number of serious accidents, and one grandchild became clinically depressed. There is no scientific way to prove that the cluster of symptoms and incidents were related to the death of the grandfather, but the timing of what transpired is a clue to the connection.

If we remain connected to our first family, we have the opportunity to process what is coming "down the generations" at its source. If we disconnect and cut off our first families, the intensity of the cutoff will create an impact somewhere else in the family system.

Dealing with Family Problems at Their Source

No one better illustrated the connection between dealing with one's family of origin issues and resolving current problems than Adrian, a twenty-eight-year-old woman from the Midwest who was an early client of mine and with whom I worked for ten months. At that time I had only begun learning about coaching and it is only in hindsight that I can appreciate the impressive work that she did with her family that year.

Adrian had come to New York City with Lonnie, her nine-year-old son from a teenage marriage that had lasted only three years. She was unhappy about a relationship she was having with a boyfriend that was "going nowhere," and she was never sure whether she was being an adequate mother to her son. Along with all of Adrian's self-doubt were her ambiguous relationships with members of her first family. She was the eldest of five siblings who were scattered around the country and only made contact with each other during Christmas. When Adrian began seeing me, she did not know the prognosis of her father's stomach cancer which had been diagnosed earlier that year, and she had minimal contact with her mother who was recently retired. Adrian insisted that there were deep emotional ties between members of her family but to all outward appearances there seemed few.

I suggested to Adrian that she might benefit from speaking to her mother and especially to her father whom she viewed as a pillar of strength, as she and I were sitting together and talking in New York. I also directed her to read *The Dance of Anger* by Harriet Goldhor Lerner, a book about family of origin work. Adrian read the book and took its message about family work much more seriously than I did, and she decided to apply what she had learned.

Adrian left New York for the summer and returned to the Midwest to spend time with her family. The next time I saw her was September of that year. When she returned to see me, it was clear that something had changed for Adrian that summer. The woman sitting in my office hardly seemed to be the same person who had come into therapy with so many loose ends a year before. She told me that she had spent that summer—a full three months—back in her hometown. During that period she spoke with her father every day. He was terminally ill but she was the only family member who would speak openly with him about his illness and his impending death. From her conversations with him she learned how he had become "the strong one" in his family, a role that she as the eldest child had also learned to play. Adrian had asked her mother to help her learn more about the family history. Since she had retired that year while caring for her husband, she welcomed the opportunity to go through the town records and the family bibles to get the birth records and other significant family information going back several generations. Adrian also asked her mother to try to recall some of the stories that went into the family history, and she got to know a great deal about what had gone on between people in her family on an emotional level.

Adrian understood that the stories her mother told her weren't facts, but they were the myths, rules, and patterns of family behavior out of which she had also evolved. She began looking at her own childhood from her mother's perspective. Adrian and her mother became a lot closer through this process.

In their later meetings as Adrian described them to me, it became clear that here was someone with a firmer sense of her own direction than I had seen before. It was clear that a major transformation was taking place, but it was not clear to me how all of this had come about.

Adrian moved to the West Coast the following spring. She had always wanted to live there but never believed she would gain the initiative to relocate. Later I received a letter from Adrian:

Dear Mr. Epstein,

Lonnie and I are now living comfortably in San Francisco. It has been relatively easy to find work as a dance instructor and I've even begun to set up a private dance therapy practice— and guess what else! I have been able to set realistic fees for clients without going through the agony that it used to cause me in the past.

I've also met a guy who I really like and who likes to hang out with Lonnie and me. I know this is a new relationship and I don't want to get my hopes up too high but this really feels right to me and I'm just so much clearer about what my own needs are. Lonnie also seems to have made a nice adjustment to San Francisco and his new school. He listens to me more than he ever did and I have been able to balance my needs with his as my son.

My father died in April and I flew in for the funeral. It was sad for me, but I also feel that I had said everything that I needed to say to him last summer. There was no unfinished business between us. I used the funeral as a time to reconnect with my brothers and sisters, and I have resolved never to allow myself to lose touch with any of them again. Mother and I now speak every week and we compare notes about being mothers and the family history of motherhood that we examined together that summer we spent together. Thank you for the work you did with me—I feel that something within me has really changed.

Warmest regards,

Adrian

After reading this letter when it first arrived I tucked it away in a drawer where I kept my clients' records. I can recall mentioning to a colleague that a client of mine who moved to the West Coast seemed to have some kind of "flight into health"—a phrase reserved for those clients who seem to get well "too quickly," and whose "cure" cannot really be trusted to last. However, I did not realize at that time something had changed Adrian during the summer she had returned home to spend time with her parents. I had been a minor player in whatever had occurred but it was years later that I was able to appreciate the profound changes she had created between herself and her family in defining a more solid sense of herself.

6

DEFINING A SELF

Each family is unique, but all families operate by certain principles. Knowing this allows us to reasonably predict what will occur in our families even when we're about to do something that challenges the usual pattern. Every activity has its set of rules, and reconnecting with your first family is no exception. Some guidelines that you should consider as you plan what has been referred to as "reentry" into your family are:

1. TRY TO PREDICT HOW FAMILY MEMBERS WILL REACT TO YOUR MOVES AND BE PREPARED TO RESPOND TO THEIR REACTIONS.

Many people find that there is no emotionally neutral territory in their first family. Supposedly innocent questions about the past can set off an emotionally charged response. When we try new ways of relating, especially by breaking an unwritten family rule, the message that we may get back is: "Stop what you're doing!" The message may emerge as anger, or it may arrive in stony silence, but it comes. Past behavior is a good indicator of present reaction. You may not know exactly what your mother or father will say or do. The way they've responded to questions or inquiries in the past is a good guide as are the demands they place on you in the present. Therefore, making a commitment to think out your position as tensions rise between yourself and others is crucial. We know that our new behavior will cause upheaval. Disappointing parental expectations is difficult, but knowing you are developing a mature approach to the past and to change is very self satisfying.

2. WHEN YOU TRY TO RECONNECT WITH YOUR MOTHER OR FATHER, THERE WILL BE SOME TROUBLE WITH THE WAY THEY HAVE ALWAYS TREATED YOU. IF YOU'RE HAVING A HARD TIME WITH YOUR FATHER, THINK ABOUT HIM WITH HIS FATHER. THERE ARE OLDER AND LARGER FAMILY PATTERNS THAT HAVE MOLDED HIM AS WELL AS YOU.

Aside from our partners, our parents can push our buttons better than anyone else in the world. If, in dealing with my father, I am only able to focus on what he has always done to me and is still doing today, then I have lost the research stance I sought when trying to understand the past, and I will soon begin to over-react. If I can expand my thinking about my father to include what it must have been like for him with *his* father, then I am once again thinking about the system that has produced both him and me.

3. TAKING A NEW POSITION WITH MEMBERS OF YOUR FIRST FAMILY AND THEN CUTTING OFF CONTACT AS THINGS BEGIN TO HEAT UP WILL NOT PRODUCE CHANGE. IF YOU ARE ABLE TO STAY IN CONTACT WITH FAMILY MEMBERS WHILE MAINTAINING YOUR NEW POSITION, THE ENTIRE FAMILY WILL TAKE A STEP IN THE DIRECTION OF EMOTIONAL GROWTH.

We all need to step back at times when things begin to feel too intense between ourselves and others. Backing away may be our emotional reaction to a situation or a relationship, but it does not move us in the direction of developing a stronger "sense of self." In order to define more of a self in our families and in the rest of our lives, we need to remain connected to members of our first family throughout the changes that result from new moves that we decide to make.

4. IF, IN YOUR WORK WITH YOUR FAMILY, YOU BEGIN TO SEE ANY MEMBER AS EITHER A VILLAIN OR A SAINT, IT MEANS THAT YOU ARE STUCK AND NEED ADDITIONAL INFORMATION.

The "angels" and the "black sheep" in the family are just people with strengths and weaknesses like everybody else. An important goal of family exploration is to get a different and more realistic picture of who these people really were and are. Our view of who *they* are is connected to how we see *ourselves*.

5. IF SOMEONE IN YOUR FAMILY IS SAID TO HAVE AN EMO-TIONAL PROBLEM, LOOK FOR WHAT IS GOING ON BETWEEN HIM AND OTHER IMPORTANT PEOPLE IN HIS LIFE.

We live in a society that has taught us to think that most problems exist inside an individual. We rarely consider that emotional problems are going on *between* people and that they are also the result of difficulties with important people in our lives.

6. AS YOU RECONNECT WITH PEOPLE FROM YOUR PAST, OBSERVE YOUR OWN REACTIONS TO WHAT IS GOING ON. YOUR LEVEL OF INTENSITY SIGNALS THE IMPOR-TANCE OF THE ISSUES AT STAKE.

The degree to which you feel hurt or angry is a measure of the significance of what is going on between you and your family. Focusing more on the self and less on what you feel others are doing to you will make you less likely to simply react to them and lose your research stance.

A Father Returns Home to Better Understand His Life

The rules of returning home to a first family remain dry and lifeless until they become instruments of change in people's lives. Anthony is a man who was able to apply what he learned in coaching sessions with me to alter the way he managed the important relationships in his life. Anthony is a policeman in a small town in Connecticut. He was referred to me by a counseling unit for public employees because of a history of alcohol abuse that had cost him his badge for a period of six months. The process of gathering information from his mother about his adoption at an early age marked the end of the secrecy that had surrounded his life. In breaking his family's "no talk" rule, he saw himself as an adult for the first time and altered the way he viewed his mother and himself.

At the time we met, Anthony was twenty-nine years old and had been married for five years. His four-year-old son, James, had recently been through a three-month separation from his father while Anthony was in an alcohol recovery center. Regular attendance at Alcoholics Anonymous meetings had given Anthony a handle on the temptations to drink that he faces and taught him how easy it is to deny his problem and return to his old patterns of drinking. Anthony drank to celebrate good times and to ease the pain of bad times. He was the precinct clown who got everybody laughing and was always the one who suggested they all go out after work for a beer. When he wasn't joking, he would be "people pleasing" in some other way. In conflict situations he was always ready to keep the peace, or as he put it, "not make waves." Yet these qualities which made him a popular guy at the station house created strife at home.

During his years of heavy drinking, Anthony's wife, Robin, had taken over all management of the household. She was the one who paid the bills, balanced the checkbook and knew where the family income was going. Anthony turned over his paycheck to her and received a small allowance for weekly expenses. He never challenged the system they had created, and Robin had become accustomed to controlling everything that went on in their home.

Anthony arrived at one session with me in a dark mood that he had never displayed before. The anger that he had kept so carefully under wraps was seeping out. He described a scene in which he was watching his son James while Robin was resting in their bedroom. At the same moment that Anthony decided to go out to the car for a stuffed animal that James was asking for, Robin returned from her nap. Immediately taking over, Robin told Anthony, "James doesn't need that teddy bear in the car. There are plenty of stuffed animals in the house for him to play with." When Anthony told Robin that he was going to get the toy anyway, Robin started yelling at him.

"What are you doing?" Robin screamed. "I said he doesn't need it!"

James looked searchingly at his father to see what he was going to do. Anthony went out to the car and brought in the teddy bear without commenting to Robin. However, he became very sullen and withdrew from Robin and James for the next few days.

At our next session, Anthony told me that he was fed up with being treated like a child by his wife and that part of him wanted to be out of the marriage altogether.

"I'm a grown man," he said, "and I've done a lot of hard work staying sober. I don't need to be put down in front of my son."

When he calmed down, I was able to point out that it had taken him and Robin many years to create a marriage in which they each maintained separate roles—Robin the parent and him the child. I told him that he could not completely blame his wife for creating this problem. I suggested that he needed to do some work on *himself* while he attempted to change their marriage and that the best place to begin was to reconnect with the family in which he grew up.

Breaking a Family Rule

Anthony related that he was adopted at birth but had never been told about it by his mother. He learned about his adoption at age ten, when he overheard some kids in the neighborhood talking about him. At that point, Anthony began to make sense out of suspicions he had felt all his life about looking different from his two brothers. By the time Anthony was fourteen, his adoptive father had left the family after many years of alcoholic binging. Anthony took over the role vacated by his father and worked hard to keep the family afloat. Although he never got to play much after his father left, he did learn to drink on the sly. At age eighteen he joined the Marines; there he consumed such large amounts of alcohol that he had two-day blackouts, could not remember anything afterward, and ended up in a military hospital. In my opinion, much of Anthony's life had been a blackout. I felt he needed to know a lot more about his connection to his past if he was ever going to piece together an effective identity in the present.

When I asked Anthony what he knew about his adoption and his birth mother, he told me that he knew nothing at all. All his life he had imagined the circumstances around his birth and his adoption, but he had never asked his mother for the facts. In the absence of facts, he imagined the worst. I told Anthony that if he truly wanted to work out his problems with his present family, he would need to obtain correct information about his past. I also told him that, when he was ready, he would need to speak to his adoptive mother about issues she and he had never discussed.

I said that I could work with him to try and figure out what made it so hard for him to talk about his adoption with his mother and why he had never raised the issue before. However, I made it clear that I would only be acting as his coach and he would be the one doing the actual work.

Many of Anthony's problems in carving out a role for himself as a husband and father were related to his position with his first family. He remained in the same position with his wife as he did with his mother: he was afraid to ask for something for himself, and he was afraid to make waves. He was unable to make any statement that would establish him as an adult, and he looked upon upsetting his mother in any way as a family crime. He knew that he was not supposed to talk about his adoption, and he had remained loyal to that injunction his entire life.

The gathering of information about who he was and where he came from meant taking a radically new stance in his family and recognizing his rights as an adult. In order to grow up, Anthony needed to break a family rule and risk upsetting his mother. Without making this change in his relationship with his first family, he would in some important way always remain a child.

During seven years on the force, Anthony had cornered a number of criminals and walked into armed robberies in progress. He was known in his precinct for his courage in dangerous circumstances. His partners never questioned that he would be there for them in life and death situations. Talking with his mother was another story. Like so many men who have grown up without learning to communicate their needs to others, Anthony was less afraid when facing physical danger than he was in opening up this emotional topic with his mother. Coaching Anthony on how to approach his mother took several months. He needed to face his own resistance in order to understand that this was not going to be a quick operation.

The following is a segment of a session with Anthony as he decides how and when he will approach his mother.

COACH: If you decided to ask your mother about your adoption, what would be a good time or place for you to bring it up to her?

ANTHONY: It would have to be a time when James and Robin weren't around. I could stop by her house Monday evening after my shift. That would be about seven-thirty and she would be finished with dinner by then.

COACH: So how do you think you might bring this up to her?

ANTHONY: I could just ask her straight out.

COACH: She might be pretty shocked since you've never brought any of this up before. People sometimes do better when you offer them a reason for why you're deciding to do something now. You're the one introducing something new in your relationship with your mother.

ANTHONY: I could tell Mom that I've been thinking more about my life and all the things that have gone on over the years. She also knows that I come to see you.

COACH: That sounds good to me. You're coming to see me for help and you're also asking her as your mother if she can help you out with a little information. Tell me how you might say it. Make believe it's Monday night and you're sitting with your mom in her living room.

ANTHONY: Mom, I've been thinking about the past and there's a lot of things I don't know about. You know I've been seeing Mr. Epstein for a while now. He thinks it would be a good idea if I learned more about my adoption and some of the things that were going on back then.

COACH: Pretty good, but if you say that your counselor wants this information, then she can question the help you're getting and not have to deal with the fact that it is you who wants to find this out for yourself. What would it be like for you to take the "I position," which makes it clear that this information is important to you?

ANTHONY: I can see how hard it is for me to ask her for anything that just has to do with me.

COACH: How do you think she'll react when you ask for this information? What will she say or do?

ANTHONY: If I say that this is something that will help me, I think she'll talk about it. I think she might start crying.

COACH: What would it be like for you if she did start crying? How might you respond?

ANTHONY: I would probably get her a cup of tea and I'd say that we could stop this for a while if she's upset.

COACH: What would it be like for you to tell her that you see that it brings up sad feelings to talk about this, but that you think that it would be important to continue?

ANTHONY: I like that. I always think I have to stop everything I'm doing as soon as anybody gets upset. It's like I'm always "people pleasing."

COACH: That sounds right. You think that feeling sad or crying about something means that you're doing something wrong and you'd better stop it. Ever think that talking about this with her might benefit both of you?

ANTHONY: How much do you think I should bring up during this visit? I've got a lot of questions about my natural mother and father and what was going on at that time.

COACH: You might not want to go for too much information the first time you bring up this topic. You'll probably get a feel for how much is too much to get into all at once. Don't forget that you may hear things that are surprising or upsetting to you. And you don't want to overload the situation by stirring up more than you or she can handle.

You might want to look at this as the first meeting that's part of a new way of you relating to your mother.

Anthony was able to approach his mother with questions about the circumstances around his adoption after carefully rehearsing his lines. He was astonished by her response. Rather than being devastated by the painful memories as he had imagined, she calmly recounted what had occurred and said that he should always "feel free to ask about the past." She then asked if he would like to speak to his uncle who had been instrumental in setting up the adoption twenty-nine years before. Eventually, Anthony was able to locate his birth mother and the adoptive father who had abandoned his family for alcohol when Anthony was young. The information that he acquired filled in some gaping holes in Anthony's knowledge about his past. In the process of asking these important questions, he took a significant new position with his mother. This new position also carried over into his marriage and his parenting relationship with his son.

Family of Origin Work and Better Fathering

Before Anthony had established his new position with his mother, his fathering lacked what I call "definition." His pattern of people pleasing got in the way of his parenting. He was a man who loved and wanted to please his son, but there were also times when I felt that he was just pacifying the boy so that he would not get upset. James needed to hear the word *no* when it was appropriate, Anthony's new ability to "make waves" and assert himself with his mother carried over into his relationship with his son. He seemed better able to take a clear position with James even though what he was asking him was not always going to please the child or avoid a scene. This, in turn, improved relations between Anthony and Robin as parents. Robin no longer felt that she was always being cast in the role of the "bad guy"—the parent who sets the limits and says no.

As time went on, Anthony was able to make waves when he needed to in his marriage. He could have a different opinion that might even be displeasing to his wife. In changing his relationship to his mother in his first family, he was able to create a different sense of "self" in all of his relationships.

Defining a Self

Anthony was better able to define his identity as a husband and father after he learned how to take clearer positions with his mother. The growth experience that Anthony went through when he did this work is called "differentiation." It is the term first used by Bowen to describe the process by which adults define who they are within the complicated network of relationships that makes up their lives. In his research with families, Bowen discovered that a person who is able to become "more of a self" in one significant relationship will reap the benefit of that change with other people in his life.

The program put forth in this book is designed to help men define a stronger sense of self. This is a process that continues over the course of our lives—it is not simply a series of events. It may, therefore, be helpful to describe the characteristics of an individual who is moving in the direction of differentiation.

You are in the process of differentiating if you are able to say who you are to important people in your life and also allow them to express who they are. You have learned to make clear statements about who you are, and you no longer insist that others have to change to suit your wishes.

In the process of differentiating, Anthony had to tolerate the anxiety that went along with stating who he was to his mother, his wife, and his child. This was very difficult for him to do, since the family script that he grew up with made it clear that doing anything that might upset his mother was unacceptable behavior. In defining more of a self, Anthony needed to stop allowing the approval or disapproval of his mother to determine what he revealed about himself.

At several points in the coaching process, I could feel Anthony pulling back. He would begin to feel that he was "pushing things" with his wife, even though he was only making minor demands. In the marital system that Anthony and Robin had created together, little changes could set off large storms. Anthony would initially take a new position with his wife, but then he would cut off from her as their conflict escalated. Coaching him during those periods involved helping him to remain in emotional contact with his wife while he took a look at the anxiety that was being set off within himself.

You are moving toward a higher level of differentiation to the degree that you are able to remain objective in emotionally charged situations involving the significant people in your life. A family member who takes a new position will almost always set off anxiety and reactions in others. But individual growth occurs only if that member does not cut off from family members while things are in a state of emotional turmoil.

Remaining clear headed and connected to the important people in your life during high stress periods may sound easy, but it is extremely hard to put into practice. It is particularly challenging to men who often complain that they have a hard time when someone becomes "too emotional." A number of men whom I have coached view themselves as "able to remain calm under pressure." Yet the calm that they refer to has to do with tensions on the job or physical challenges and danger. In the family arena, each of the men I coached had learned to "keep his cool" by tuning out his wife. When things heated up emotionally between them and their partners, the men reduced the tension by withdrawing and cutting off communication. Each of these men needed to learn to tolerate his anxiety as tensions rose and also to observe his own part in the emotional process. In order to define more of a self, they needed to be able to sustain a dialogue with their wives within the intense emotional field of marital disagreements and conflicts.

Stop Overreacting!

If the process of differentiation has to do with bringing a stronger sense of self to life situations, then reactivity refers to those behaviors that do not move us toward personal growth and development. When we know that we are overreacting to something, we are usually in a no-growth position. Ron Richardson, a leader in the field of coaching, has defined four reactive positions that come out of our anxiety and feelings of powerlessness.

First is the "one-up" position. Have you ever gotten into a conflict that sounds like this? She says, "You're going to do *that*? Well, I'll do one better." Not to be outdone, you respond, "You think you're going to do me one better? Well, I'll show you!"

Some of the couples I've worked with seem locked into reactive positions in which everything one partner says or does becomes the basis for the other partner's next move. They are both trapped in their behaviors. They are only able to react to the other and are not able to stay focused on the self. A less reactive, more differentiated position would be a "deal" that one of the partners makes with himself. For instance, a differential position sounds something like this monologue:

"I've made an agreement with myself not to argue or curse in front of the children. Whether or not my partner pushes my buttons, I'm going to maintain my position."

Next is the rebellious position. The rebel often bases much of his identity on being *against* someone or something. To others, this may even seem like he knows where he stands on issues. The rebel's sense of self hinges on an exterior force against which he can react. During my own rebellious period in adolescence and young adulthood, I thought I was taking important positions in the name of my "cause." Actually, I was participating in a system of action and reaction between myself and the authorities. I usually ended the day more focused on the evil authority figures than the cause I thought I was trying to promote. Rebelling against the authorities temporarily protected me from having to take a look at my lack of a solid sense of self.

The third reactive position is the compliant position. The person in this stance just goes along with someone else's wishes without making it clear where he stands. Many fathers are compliant with their wives and refuse to take clear positions on family issues. A more thorough description of the compliant father occurs later in this book.

Last is the emotionally cut off position. In cutting off, partners in a relationship decide to end communication with each other. By the time a person has cut himself off from an important person in his life, he may feel that he has done everything possible to make things better between them. Breaking off communication is usually thought to be a last resort, in which the person cutting the connection may feel justified in making this decisive move.

In terms of defining more of a self, cutoffs are viewed as extremely reactive positions that indicate high levels of tension between the involved parties. I have been told the story of two brothers in my mother's family. One brother was supposed to bring the milk to a family gathering. When he showed up without the milk, he and his brother got into a conflict that resulted in them not communicating for the next twelve years. Since this cutoff was obviously about more than forgotten groceries, it would be important to know what else had been going on in the family that might have caused their behavior.

Cutoffs don't happen because people do not matter to one another. They actually signify both the importance of a particular relationship and the degree of unresolved intensity contained within its emotional borders. An unfortunate result of cutoffs in families is the loss of opportunity for the self to develop in that branch of the family. The intensity that leads to cutoffs may come down the generations from older, unresolved conflicts from the past. And the tensions that they produce can create problems for generations to come.

7

ENTERING
THE FAMILY
EMOTIONAL FIELD

I HAVE ALWAYS KNOWN that my ongoing anger was an echo of a voice from my past. I have also known that the voice I was hearing was my father's—just as he had heard his own father's angry voice. The intensity of the anger that I felt rarely fit the situation I was in, and the people who came into contact with me became aware that I had some unknown problem and stepped back.

I believe that in unconscious, patterned ways, we all carry the behaviors, beliefs, desires, and feelings of the generations that have preceded us. I have also come to understand that the more we try to distance ourselves from those figures and their memories, the greater the probability is that we will pass along their character traits to our children and the generations to come. There is warmth and humor in my father's family, qualities that I would like my children to develop. But there is also a dark side to the men in my father's family that I wanted to better understand and finally put to rest.

This is the story of how I returned to my first family in order to come to terms with the problems I was having in other areas of my life. In some ways, it is the story of my growing into adulthood and my ability to become the father that I always wanted but never had.

I am sad to say that by the time I came to understand the importance of reconnecting with my father, he had been gone for eighteen years. I was only twenty-three when he died, and his death occurred during a period in my life when I was completely cut off from members of my first family. I did not think much about my father at the time, and I dismissed his memory as a part of my life that I had left behind. Beneath my denial of his importance there existed a fury about the father image that he had not provided and the man I had always wanted him to be. He had always seemed passive. I accepted this outwardly but inwardly I was silently pleading for him to act. He withdrew from our family in ways that left an emotional vacuum that I was predestined to fill. In looking back, I am not sure if I paid a greater price for his withdrawal from me as a child or from my later decision to remain distant from him as a young man. I guess we both paid heavily for what we could have given to each other and did not. Yet, I continued to believe for many years that he had made little impact on my life. If I had been able to look a little closer and a little deeper, I would have understood that every aspect of my life was a reflection of his way of being—from the conflicts I had in my failed first marriage, to the hostile relationships I had created with my supervisors at my job. I was reacting to his memory without the slightest awareness of it. Meanwhile I was acting out family scenes in my own life.

My Own Journey Home

Nevertheless, I was aware that my own life was unsatisfying and because of this I began to reconnect to the people in my past.

The experience of renewed contact and conversations with family members who were important to my father when he was alive awakened strong feelings in me. At times, it felt like I had reconnected with him in some way, or that I had entered into what I can only describe as an "emotional field." I began to have vivid memories of him and he seemed to come alive in my dreams. As I look back at this period, I see my reactions as a part of the powerful emotional "circuitry" that exists between family members. The person who elicited the strongest feelings and memories about my father was my mother.

Part of me has always known that I needed to speak to my mother, and another part of me resisted approaching her for many years. I had always talked *about* my mother in therapy or with close friends, but I had never spoken *with* her about her life before I was born or the experiences that shaped her personality and beliefs. I had also never inquired about my father's past to discover what made him into the passive but volatile man he was.

During my initial visit to the small suburban home where I grew up, my mother prepared a dinner for me and I did a few chores. She was not one to speak about the past or any potentially emotional topic, and I also steered clear of approaching areas that might prove intense.

There was one period back when I was in therapy that I decided to "confront" my mother and describe all I felt I had not received emotionally as a child. Predictably, she responded by enumerating everything she felt she had given up for me as I grew up. I learned little about myself or my family from that encounter, except that criticism of a parent will probably be met with a defensive response.

It was only after I learned more about families as emotional systems that I was able to adopt a more objective and less reactive stance in my relationship with my mother. I disciplined myself to avoid overtones of criticism or blame toward her, and the tenor of our communication immediately changed from defensive posturing to shared stories and information. It was during this period that I was able to reap the benefits of my mother's knowledge about our family. One night, we sat down in the living room with the family photo albums in front of us and I asked questions about her memories and perceptions. Her answers gave me new perspectives on what I had once accepted as fact. I learned about her father's escape from the tsar's armies following the Kishniev pogroms in 1903, his passage to Canada, and his arrival in Manhattan's Lower East Side. I felt my first emotional connection to a generation of immigrants who had come to a new land to escape prejudice, but who had lost contact with their own parents left behind in cities and tiny villages in the Ukraine. I began to understand the context of my mother's childhood and family life, which was framed for me by new knowledge about the era in which she grew up. The Great Depression and the rise of Fascism in Europe took on new meanings in this context. It was at this point that I began to work on my family genogram. A genogram is a family tree that tracks a family's emotional connections as well as its births, deaths, marriages, and divorces. It is an important tool in the coaching process, and it has helped me to understand my place in the larger family system. (For an explanation of how to construct a family genogram, see the Appendix at the end of this book.) What I learned about myself while speaking with my mother went beyond the facts that I gathered.

Learning to Accept My Parents as Different from Myself

Of course, I am different from my parents. Over the course of my life I had devoted a considerable amount of energy to proving just how different I was. I had said to myself, "I will never bring up my children the way they brought me up."

Yet, in my conversations with my mother, I experienced difficulty accepting what she chose to tell me and the way she communicated her ideas. It was different from what I wanted to hear. She told me about the sights and sounds of the Lower East Side and gave me a factual account of the lives of her four older brothers. I appreciated that, but I also wanted her to describe the emotional connections between her family members and some of the anguish that all families experience as they go through the life cycle. I asked her, but she would not tell me. It was something that I felt myself react negatively to, which only meant that I needed to give it more thought.

I am a product of the 1960s and 1970s, decades in which people began to speak more openly about problems that were once thought too personal to share with others. Psychotherapy became the norm in some circles, and it was considered a virtue to open up and connect with people in an emotional way. By contrast, my mother is a product of the 1920s, the Great Depression, and World War II. She looks at the world and her personal connections in a different way from mine. In her view, one only presents what is going well in one's life and keeps the rest to oneself. Her motto is, "What's happened in the past is done. Why would anyone want to bring up past conflicts or the skeletons in the family closet?"

In her family, you did not discuss your feelings openly with others. It was a closed emotional system with strict rules about how much was communicated to outsiders. In my career as a therapist, I have daily conversations with outsiders about the most intimate details of their lives. The thing that I considered most important to do—to speak about and understand the family emotional system with all of its problems—was the very thing that my mother considered taboo. But it was not for me to get my mother to change her way of being, any more than it was my mother's responsibility to make sure that I saw the world her way. I later understood that, in many ways, my mother's way of handling her emotional life worked for her in the same way that I felt openness worked for me. Her way wasn't wrong. It was just different.

Learning to appreciate differences between ourselves and other people in our lives is a benchmark of our personal development. If I can be who I am without insisting that others change to accommodate me, then I have achieved a higher level of selfhood.

In her book *The Dance of Intimacy,* Harriet Lerner puts it this way: "Our goal is to have relationships that do not occur at the expense of the self, and a self that does not operate at the expense of others."

Revelations

As I continued to visit and speak with my mother about her life and memories, I began to ask her about the life of my father and his family. He was not alive to answer questions or to refute my mother's perceptions, and his early ties were even more shrouded in mystery than her own. His unpredictable tirades and jealous feelings were the legacy of our emotional bond, but this was my first attempt at understanding the emotional system that produced these traits.

As my mother talked to me of my father, she related a story she had been told by him about Raizel Begun, my father's mother. My father had never shared it with me. According to her account, my paternal grandmother was a woman who suffered from delusional episodes. She believed that her husband was involved with the woman in the apartment below, as well as other women around their Lower Manhattan neighborhood. Whether or not my grandfather was a faithful husband and whether there were aspects to his personality that might have made his wife doubt him, I would learn later in conversations with my aunt. The story was never substantiated or refuted by facts. Nevertheless, to me, it was an important revelation and a vital piece of the family emotional puzzle. I thought back to the angry jealous scenes that I had witnessed as a child and was able to place them in context. Those awful moments were not something that my father wittingly subjected me to: they were a repeat performance of behavior he had witnessed in his own life. The behavior that I always hated and feared had not magically appeared in my father's psyche. It was connected to his own family relationship. It was part of the emotional history that had been passed from earlier generations to both of us.

Hearing the story of jealousy and mistrust in my grandparents' marriage marks for me the beginning of my personal odyssey into the emotional history of my family. It is not a history recorded in books but one in which I am the daily participant as well as an observer. As I worked on understanding this, it became clear to me that I am not an isolated psychological particle hurtling through emotional space. I am part and parcel of an emotional network that has taken many generations to evolve. My growth as an individual, and as a father in particular, has very much to do with my understanding of this system and playing my adult role as it too continues to evolve.

8

THE SINS
OF THE FATHERS

I am a jealous God visiting the sins of the fathers upon the children unto the third and fourth generation.

Exodus 20:5

FOR FATHERS, I BELIEVE the process of defining the self is a matter of redefining who we are as men. When I chose not to repeat the pattern of my father's life, I knew I would have to learn even more about the men who preceded me in my family system. The information from my mother helped me to piece together the puzzle of his jealous moods, but I still needed to learn more about his threatening gestures and angry outbursts. Teasing, hitting, intimidation and violent behaviors are part of the darker legacy of my father's family. They are closely tied to the anger and resentment I have harbored for much of my life.

There are many therapeutic "prescriptions" for healing the effect of parental violence against children. Some therapists encourage their adult clients to confront their parents about past abuse in the hope of "empowering" the person who felt quite helpless as a child. Other therapists suggest role playing in which the client imagines the abusive parent to be seated in front of him. In this safe environment, the client gets to shout any words of protest he wants to his abusive parent. Just talking to a trained professional or a close friend about past violence can help focus the victim's sense of outrage and neutralize the anger felt about childhood violations. I have tried all of these approaches and have found them to be cathartic, but insufficient for healing.

My healing from the effects of family violence began when I reconnected with members of my extended family. Conversations with an aunt and several cousins broadened my view and revealed a pattern of abuse that had existed between fathers and sons in my family for generations, and in a country more than 8000 miles away.

The first relative, other than my mother, to whom I spoke about family violence was my Aunt Edith. She was the wife of my father's youngest brother and the only living adult from his generation who knew the family well enough to help me. She was able to verify events from my childhood that I could not have confirmed without her assistance.

Validation

I have distinct memories of my father chasing me through the house when I was seven or eight. The memories end with me cowering in the bathroom. The bathroom was the only room in my house that had a latch on the door, but I was forbidden to use it. Therefore, I was left defenseless against the beating that followed. The terror of being stalked by my father was always worse than the pain of being struck, but the event became a ritual with a role for every member of the family.

I have hazy memories of times when my father struck me in a random manner that seemed disconnected from any infraction that I may have committed. I recall feeling that I must have done something bad to bring on such a reaction from him—I just couldn't figure out what it was. I have other vague memories of early family gatherings when all was going well until something erupted that left me the target of my father's sudden, arbitrary rage.

My aunt's recollections became an important part of my attempt to reconstruct some of these events. She told me stories about how difficult it was to live with her own husband, and how unpredictable his anger was. The similarities between her husband and my father were obvious. In our later discussions, she described a family get-together in my backyard when I was about eight and her own daughter Joan was ten. She recalled that Joan and I were playing on the lawn and laughing together when for no apparent reason my father grabbed me and threw me to the ground in front of everyone. One moment all seemed okay, and the next I was being subdued and humiliated. I recalled that afterward I ran out of the backyard and down an alley. I cannot remember where I ran, but I knew that I didn't want anyone to see me and needed to hide.

My aunt sadly described this scene. She apologized for having been unable to rescue me from my father at the time, and confessed she was also frightened of the men in our family. Her own husband was no less a bully than his older brother. Was my father trying to show his family the strict control he had over his son, or was he unwittingly repeating a family pattern in which he had participated in his own childhood? I did not understand his reasons. However, even at such a young age, I was already storing up my own reservoirs of rage which I would later let loose in new situations and new relationships.

I was moved by my aunt's pain as she shared her memories and her regrets with me. I felt close to her and thanked her for validating what I thought had occurred, but could not confirm without her memories.

Conversations with My Cousin

The little girl who had been playing with me in my backyard the day my father struck me was my first cousin Joan. When
I thought about how much I liked her and all that we had in common, it seemed strange that we'd hardly spoken in the forty years
since that frightening event. In recent years we have reestablished
contact. Joan has also developed curiosity about our family and
its patterns.

During our conversations I learned of an uncanny similar-
ity between my cousin's emotional experience and my own. She
also grew up with the unsettling feeling that her life could be
thrown into turmoil without warning. When I asked her if her
father had told her stories about growing up in his family, she
said that he had given her some strong impressions but little specific information. He did convey that his family had an extremely
harsh emotional environment and that he was expected to "be
tough" and learn to "take it." He told her that he was teased a lot
in his family. I later came to see that teasing was an important
part of "learning to be a man in the Epstein family." It was a
theme that came up again in other contexts.

My cousin remembers her father as a warm and even nurturing man at times, which drew her to him. But as much as she
wanted to be close to her father, his unpredictable anger and
explosiveness created an emotional distance between them.

I began to see that the relationship between fathers and
daughters in my extended family was quite different from what
transpires between fathers and sons. Unlike my distant relationship with my father, Joan has always felt closer and identified
more with her father than her mother. This is much the same way
that my sister has described her perceptions of her own relations
with our family. However, neither woman has been able to get
past her father's wall of anger to forge an emotional bond with her
male parent. Conversely, when I met with Joan's older brother,

Harry, he told me that he remembers nothing about the anger and turbulence that went on in his childhood, while his mother can recount incident upon incident of father-son abuse.

Not only do family members often have different recollections of events from the past, they may manage their emotional reactions to these events in very different ways. If the emotional experience has been extremely intense, a family member may cut off from the memory itself. This type of cutoff can place the next generation of that family at greater risk.

The Pattern Continues

One incident that my cousin Joan related to me gave me an awesome sense of the pervasive pattern of father violence in our ancestors. She described being a teenager and going to work with her father. It was the type of experience that young children look forward to with the anticipation of discovering what Daddy's life is like when he is not at home. My uncle introduced his daughter to the women who worked with him in the office that he managed. She hadn't been there very long when her father, suddenly and without apparent reason, gave her a hard smack across the face. At first she went into emotional shock from the unanticipated violence. Then she felt a sense of shame and humiliation. In her disorientation, she wasn't able to ask her father what she had done to cause his attack.

My cousin tried to convey to me how distraught and totally helpless she felt after this incident. I told her she didn't have to describe it: I already knew the feeling too well.

This was also the case with another cousin, a thirty-two-year-old man from Israel who called me while on a business trip in the United States. He ended up staying in my house for a week. Actually, his visit did not happen entirely by chance, since I had been corresponding with his father and trying to establish connections with this little-known branch of my family.

My paternal grandfather was born in Russia in 1871 and had two younger brothers. My grandfather and the next oldest brother emigrated to America at the turn of the century. The youngest brother, Ezekiel, a carpenter like my grandfather, had always been the religious one in the family and felt it was his mission as a Jew to settle in what he considered the "Promised Land." According to my cousin, Ezekiel was always teased by his brothers for his pious nature. (It is significant that my cousin mentioned this to me, since the tormenting of sons seems a family tradition.) In 1925, Ezekiel traveled with his wife and five children from Pinsk to Palestine and settled in what is now Tel Aviv. After his first wife died, he married again and had four sons from this second union. Ezekiel died in 1950, and it is from his youngest son, Isaac, and grandson Zack that I gathered most of my information about this branch of my family.

Some of my curiosity about my Israeli cousins stemmed from the fact that this generation of my father's family had split off from one another. It was interesting to me that two brothers came to America while the youngest decided, because of his religious convictions, to settle in what was the future Jewish homeland. I wondered if he was a more spiritual man than his older brother and less prone to the rage that so characterized the other men in the family.

My cousin Zack, who fortuitously dropped in on me, was warm and open and was willing to sit down with me and figure out what had been going on in the emotions of our family over the generations. As he began to describe the relationship he had with his parents, I started to have the feeling that I was hearing a familiar story. Zack said he had never been beaten as a child. He described his father as a liberal man who believed that he "could get along with anyone." Yet, underneath this mild facade, his father could be angry and temperamental. Like my own father, his father withdrew into himself. Similar to me, my cousin had also filled the emotional void left by a father who was not present in spirit. He, too, was trying to let go of the burdens from his past.

As Zack and I sat in front of the family photographs that I had taken out, I asked him questions about his grandfather that had been on my mind since I began to think about my family in Israel. Was he a different type from my grandfather? Had he treated his sons more kindly? The answers my cousin gave me about his grandfather were disturbing. Unfortunately, they confirmed what I was beginning to understand about families and the emotional patterns that seem to be repeated over time.

He told me that his father spoke very little about his childhood with Ezekiel, but the little he said portrayed a man with a vicious temper who regularly beat his youngest son. As with my family, beating was a form of social control, and the sons paid heavily for their father's wrath. Then my cousin related a story his father had told him that truly amazed me. When Zack's father was about eight years old, he was sitting at a family gathering in a chair that faced away from his father. Suddenly, he felt a blow to the back of his head that practically knocked him from the chair. The boy had no idea why his father struck him, and he was too frightened to question his father and probably risk another blow. The arbitrary violence that Joan told me about and that I personally had experienced by age seven had occurred in my family more than fifty years ago in another part of the world. As in my case and that of my female cousin, this other incident occurred in front of people and came without warning. As time went by, the beatings continued as Isaac began to expect them. When he was fifteen, his mother was dying of kidney failure and he spent a great deal of time at her bedside. One day, Ezekiel, immersed in his own grief and pain, decided once again that his son was being disobedient and needed a lesson. He raised his hand to strike his son, but by this time Isaac was six-foot-one and towered over his father. He caught his father's fist in midair and forced the older man's arm painfully downward.

The victory for Isaac was a shallow one. As he looked into his father's defeated eyes, he felt only grief and shame. Ezekiel never struck Isaac again.

Understanding the Legacy

Family members have an unlimited amount of information to pass on and numerous stories to tell. The stories that we select about our families are always important ones. They convey something essential about the way we see our families and ourselves.

There are other violent scenes that have been imprinted in the minds of my aunt and my cousins, and there are remarkable similarities in each of these experiences to scenes in my own childhood.

Like my cousins, I had grown up in the shadow of my father's anger and pain. The legacy of family violence extends further than I ever imagined. The stories that my cousins related to me about our family history have caused me to pause and reflect on the problems that I have also struggled with in my relationship with my children. I have never struck my children or even raised my hand in a violent gesture. However, when I think back to the time when I was painting benches with them, I remember the rush of anger within me that I could never understand. The feeling was arbitrary, irrational, and connected to a family emotional process that I was just beginning to grasp.

Later, as I reconnected with my first family, I came to feel that I also had to face the fact that I lived with a family legacy of male anger and violence that has involved teasing, beatings, and public humiliation. At times it was a random anger that rose up and attacked other people, especially children, when they least expected it. At other moments, memories of harsh words and cold stares were the legacies I bore. I had always hated what my father did to me, but I learned that father violence has been passed from generation to generation to infect my family, to infect me.

After years of intensive self-scrutiny in conventional psychotherapy on what I had always viewed as my "personal" problems, I finally began getting myself out of the central position. I examined a larger family history with all of the secrets, skeletons, and reflections of my own issues over several generations. It was the difference between first looking through the narrow lens of a microscope and then viewing everything blown up on a wide angle screen of family events and history.

The important consideration for my children and myself is that the information that I gathered and the stories that I heard changed the way I felt and reacted. From that time on, when I felt my own anger rise, I reflected on the other men in my family and the stories that I had heard. I had become knowledgeable about my family patterns of behavior. My new awareness helped me to ensure that I would not repeat the destructive patterns of the past. Your own search will, I hope, bring the same positive realization to you.

BECOMING YOUR OWN
MAN IN YOUR FAMILY

IN THE LAST CHAPTER we examined the ways in which a father's family of origin may be used as a vehicle for self-development, but what about making direct changes in the way we operate as husbands and fathers? Men are often accused of coming home to their wives and children but leaving part of themselves back at the office. This chapter will examine how we fare in our present families and how we can bring a stronger sense of self into our relationships with our partners and children. However, before we try to change ourselves, it will be helpful to take a look at the way we have been taught to view our personal freedom in the face of our obligations to others.

The Demands of the Job

Anthony has spent the past twenty-seven years on the assembly line at an automobile plant. He began as a welder after high school, and, except for a three-month layoff in 1977, he has never left the plant. For the past five years he's been thinking about getting out and opening a mom and pop grocery store in his town. His buddy Joe also began work at the same plant at age eighteen. And just three years ago he was promoted to foreman. At first Joe enjoyed his new status, but now he resents having to respond to pressures from the front office. He has his own ideas about how to raise productivity and he feels he has only token input into plant decision-making. Joe has been talking to Anthony about changing jobs, but he just doesn't know where else to go.

"Becoming your own man" is the way author Daniel Levenson has characterized the milestone that men try to achieve during the mid-part of their lives. This milestone may be accomplished by finally opening up a business only dreamed about for years, or it may express itself in some other new venture or change of job. However, "Becoming your own man" always seems to involve not having to answer to someone else's needs. The idea of becoming your own man may feel like salvation to those men who have spent their days "in the field," or even "in the front office," while having to respond to the demands of some organization. And yet, for many men, the wish for greater independence that comes with maturity is often expressed to family members as "Leave me alone," or "I need to get away." Far too often and for many of us, the idea of independence means disconnection from our families. It seems that we, as men, have lost touch with the link between becoming our own man and our families.

The Fear of Losing Our Freedom

There are many ages in our lives when we may feel a need to hold on to what we call our "freedom." I can recall experiencing that feeling before I got married and again when my wife and I talked about having children. Marriage and family were both things that I wanted. Yet I couldn't escape the fear that I was going to have to give something up in the process. In my anxiety over losing my "freedom," I had also lost sight of what I would gain.

The most common relationship problem that men present to me in counseling is "pressure" from a partner. This is usually related to the "pursuer-distancer" pattern in which one partner demands more time together and greater intimacy while the other feels smothered and asks for "breathing space." It is almost always the woman who requests closeness, while her husband or boyfriend asks, "What does she want from me?"

Why is it that women are so frequently the high intimacy need partners in relationships while men are left feeling the pressure of their partner's emotional demands?

The Price of Our "Manhood"

When I was growing up, the mystique that surrounded manhood had little to do with "settling down" and everything to do with being free and "untamed." A "real" man was thought to be a free man out on his own, in search of adventure. The idea of being "tied down" came dangerously close to being "tied to a mother's apron strings." The romantic figure of the "wanderer" offered an alternative image of a man who had power over women by not allowing women to have any hold over him. "Wandering" may work for some teenagers who feel they need to have a variety of experiences but it can never work for adults who would like to establish enduring relationships and stable families.

There is a price attached to men who view their "freedom" and "true masculine identity" as being apart from their family roles. This view condemns men to being the outsider and the "second parent" with lower status than their wives. Unfortunately, these men have less information about what is going on in their families and less input into family decision-making. Ultimately, many end up with less of a sense of self and diminished self-esteem.

An important question for many men to consider is:

"Why don't we feel as 'free' at home with our families as we do in other parts of our lives?"

One possible answer to this question is that we are less sure of who we are in our families and more comfortable in our roles at work.

Men tend to overfunction at work and underfunction in the home.

"Underfunctioning" in the home means not participating as an equal in those activities which have to do with family life. The diminished role that we, as men, so often play in our families is socially conditioned. Family relationships have historically been the domain of women. Men, the emotional outsiders, have paid a high price for equating their sense of identity with their jobs. We have been conditioned to value breadwinning over intimate relationships as the measure of our manhood. If we had been taught to measure our success by the quality of our connections to others instead of our income, then our people skills would probably be better than they are. As it now stands, women generally are better at the art of establishing intimacy and managing relationships. Having been raised to value connections between themselves and others, women are better positioned to define who they are than men.

More Work, Less Self

Generally men, as a group, possess less of a solid sense of self than women. This may be a bold generalization which can never be proven but I feel that it reflects the different conditions under which the majority of men and women live their lives. The way that boys are brought up generally discourages them from developing the parts of themselves that have to do with expressiveness, insight, and intimacy which are the building blocks of human connection. Instead, they have been encouraged to go outside of the home to do things—men go to work and manipulate objects or people. By removing us from the hub of interpersonal connection, we are cheated out of the primary arena in which the self is developed—the intimate network of family relationships.

Girls usually grow up with a "circle of friends" within a female culture that promotes communication, mutual support, intimacy, and the expression of feeling. Conversely, boys become ensnared early in their preparation for the outside position of the provider, protector, and procreator. Our gender education tells us to focus on keeping score while also knowing where we stand in terms of power and authority. If a solid sense of self is formed primarily in our closeness to others, then we as men have suffered a great injustice by being told to seek our identity outside of the emotional life of the family.

Most of the men who have come to see me for counseling felt that they were doing quite a good job of figuring out what they wanted for themselves in life. However, some were thinking about their own needs for the first time and were no longer content with merely being the breadwinner. Upon closer examination, I found that a number of my male clients had developed outside interests, but had not given much thought to what they wanted for themselves in their more intimate relationships. The part of their lives that had to do with identity and their needs remained confusing, uncharted territory. One teacher with whom I worked kept trying to get his girlfriend to "fit into" his life. He was sure that if she got "too close" or if he got "too involved" with her, the independent life that he had worked so hard to create would be ruined. He knew how to keep his distance when he felt they were getting too involved, but he was unable to negotiate in an open discussion with his partner the amount of togetherness and separateness that he wanted.

We, as men, can't define a self in isolation from others, and yet we often feel pressured when we are asked to clarify what we want from our marriages and how we intend to play our role as fathers. If our partners ask for something more in the way of emotional commitment than we feel we are prepared to give, we may become even more uncomfortable. As a group, we tend to shy away from intimacy in our key relationships, and we often miss the opportunity for closeness and support in other parts of our lives.

A study that examined the daily communication patterns between women would probably reveal a high level of mutual support and intimate knowledge about each other's lives. Most likely, a similar study of men's lives would indicate minimal intimate conversation with others and little emotional support. Men who experience a marital crisis often feel isolated and depressed. If our support networks are important components of our emotional health, then most men fall outside of the safety net. We tend to overload our marriages with needs that could best be served by expanding our connections with others.

Everyone has a need for both separateness from others and togetherness, but the process of defining who we are as husbands and fathers goes on within the intense emotional arena of our significant relationships.

The Problems Associated with Being a Son

Early on, men learn to be emotionally disconnected from people in their role as sons in the family. The family is a training ground for the way we behave as husbands and fathers. Although each family is unique, sons have occupied much the same position in their families for many generations. The son's position in an intact family is usually between his mother and father as depicted in the triangle on the following page.

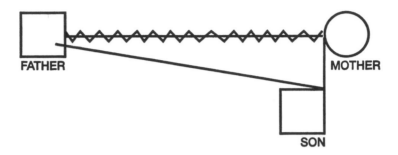

As the diagram shows, the father is in a distant, outside position, removed from his wife and his son. Even if he would like to close the "intimacy gap" between himself and his wife, he doesn't have the skills to do so. The marriage, represented by the horizontal line between husband and wife, may remain emotionally flat or hostile over many years. Under these conditions, one of the children will be "recruited" to fill the unmet needs of the parents. Either a son or a daughter may end up in the role of "emotional husband" or wife to a needy parent. However, I have found that sons end up in an even more vulnerable position than daughters when they assume this role in their families. Girls are expected to remain close to their mothers over the course of their lives, and an intense mother-daughter relationship is considered normal in our society. The wounding of sons occurs when they feel pressure to separate from their mothers and venture forth into the world outside of the family. There is an expectation for preadolescent boys to become "independent" from mother without any other involved figure to identify with and bond. The father or "circle of men" needed to nurture the developing son and provide a lighted path into manhood is usually not available. Therefore, the young boy begins to experience an emotional void.

Much of the research and literature concerning the rise of crime and violent behaviors in male teenagers during the last forty years points to the emotionally absent father as a central factor.

Things My Father Never Taught Me

I have described my father as easily angered and potentially explosive when I was in his presence. When he was with
my mother and, particularly when he was having a conflict with
her, I noticed an entirely different behavior. I can recall an
instance when they argued. My father backed down entirely from
his original point. He would grumble about my mother "always
having to be 100 percent right." I can never remember him standing by his original opinion.

Even more than his unpredictable anger, I resented his
unwillingness to take a position on anything. He never took a
stand in his own behalf, and, even when his wife berated him, he
seemed to have no "bottom line" of behaviors that he refused to
tolerate. Like so many men of his generation, he followed the
emotional path of least resistance culminating in his eventual
withdrawal or his rage.

My father lacked the skill and motivation to take meaningful positions in his marriage and stick to them in the face of
his wife's predictable resistance. Had he been able to do so, he
might have brought about change in his marriage and developed
a more solid sense of himself. As it turned out, he handed the
mantle of passivity and resentment down to me his son.

The Skills We Need at Home

There are some basic skills that most men need to develop
in order to move from the "outsider" position to a more central
place in the lives of their families. One of these is the ability to
make decisions involving family members and the other is the
capacity to negotiate differences of opinion with our partners.
This may sound simple, but it is the most challenging and important part of our personal development.

Many of the men whom I have counseled are competent decision makers and negotiators while at work, but run into difficulty when the same skills are called for in their intimate relationships. Husbands and wives will often complain that they can discuss things more easily with people other than their partners. An explanation for this is:

The intensity of the "emotional field" that exists between husbands, wives and children makes it difficult to keep the thinking part of our minds operating clearly when the anxiety level is high. There is a tendency to let go of thinking and just react emotionally to what we feel is going on.

Two crucial skills for men to develop are the ability to take clear, well-thought out positions in our important relationships and the capacity to remain calm, clearheaded and connected to the people in our lives during periods of emotional intensity and crisis.

Implicit in taking a position is that you have sufficient information for the position to be valid, and that it fits together with your values and beliefs. Strong positions in life rarely come without life experiences that have allowed us to arrive at some independent ideas about how we see the world. Clear positions are not rigid positions and they allow for changes as new information becomes available.

Bringing More Self to the System

As I considered the process of defining an identity as a father in my own family, I attempted to remain both clearheaded and emotionally available during conflicts between my wife and my elder daughter. It was the type of situation that rarely occurs in my family, and I was challenged to arrive at a satisfactory position for myself on a complicated emotional playing field. I came home late one night after seeing clients to find my wife and my teenage daughter locked in a conflict. As soon as I came through the door, my wife complained that my daughter was being arrogant and refused to acknowledge that her behavior had been disrespectful. My wife demanded my support as her partner, and asked me to join her in chastising our daughter. It seemed clear to me that in this emotionally charged climate, any attempt I made to hear my daughter's side of the story would be construed as a lack of support by my wife. My daughter looked like she was about to become even more upset if she didn't have an opportunity to air her version of the events of the evening. I was aware that I had just been recruited as the third side of a family triangle.

Triangles occur when the intensity between two people becomes too heated for them to contain. At that point, they will begin to pull in a third person who will reduce the tension between the original pair.

Finding an Acceptable Position

Part of me wished that I had stayed at my office where I might have escaped this "no-win" family scene, but the adult part of me knew that it was important to think out a responsible position in this difficult situation.

After taking some time to think about what I would do next, I decided to extricate myself from the middle ground between my wife and daughter while I remained in contact with each of them. I suggested to my wife that she might want to work out her conflict with our daughter without my participation since I hadn't been a part of it from the outset. Also, I told her that I would support her decision to impose a discipline measure if she felt our daughter had stepped too far out of line. Then, I approached my daughter and said that I would listen to her account of what had transpired between her and her mother, but that she would have to work this conflict out with her mother without my input. Finally, I let her know that I would support her mother's decision to impose a punishment if she felt that it was warranted.

I felt satisfied with the way I had handled what had originally felt like an impossible situation. I had been able to think out a responsible position for myself when things were in emotional turmoil, and "de-triangle" without cutting myself off from family members.

The Compliant Father

One of the easiest patterns that we can fall into as fathers is one of passivity. Often, we go along with the wishes of our wives and children without trying to figure out where we stand. This role may be reinforced by our outsider position in which we end up depending on our partners to fill us in on what is going on with our children. Taken to its negative extreme, a compliant father can become the "heavy" in the family, who is expected to impose discipline when his wife complains about the children's behavior. The children then fear their father and he remains an emotional outsider in the system. A father who has gotten stuck in this role begins to feel that other people are always pushing his buttons, and he may continue to look outside of himself to fix whatever he feels isn't working.

This is all part of what is called emotional reactivity, in which people act on their feelings without taking clear, thought-out positions on where they stand. The emotional reactivity that goes on in families can take the form of hostile arguments or passive resentment, but it always involves the lack of a solid sense of self. The most extreme reactive position is the emotional cut-off in which a person breaks off all communication with a family member. Although it may seem like a powerful move to the person who gets cut off, the one who has broken his ties usually feels weak and helpless underneath.

The compliant father may initially seem agreeable. However, he is conforming out of a lack of self-definition rather than a spirit of good will. If he has not thought out where he stands on issues and he is just trying to please his wife, the situation will eventually "go wrong." Since the compliant father never clearly chooses what he wants, he will eventually have to show the family that he is really disappointed and angry under the surface. If the compliant father could learn to say what he thought and negotiate openly with the important people in his life, he would move away from reactivity in the direction of defining more of a self.

Learning to Focus on the Self

Joe first came to see me for marriage counseling with his wife, Sue. Sue presented Joe as a husband who was moody and at times even explosive. In her words, "He was a man who ran hot and cold." After several counseling sessions, I came to understand Joe as someone who at first went along with whatever his wife wanted. Later, he became quite angry. When they were first married, Sue thought of her husband as "easy going," but as time went by she understood that behind the relaxed facade was a man who seethed with resentment and felt that others were always taking advantage of him. As Joe and Sue worked with me in counseling, they were able to revise the way they related to one another. Joe was able to take more responsibility for stating clearly what he wanted, and Sue learned to ask Joe a lot of questions, helping him to clarify what his wishes might be. Tensions calmed down in their marriage, but Joe continued to get very angry whenever he spent time alone with their two children.

Joanne was eight years old and Marcus was five when their parents sought counseling with me. When I saw the family together for one session, I hadn't noticed anything unusual about either of the children. It was Joe who went along with their wishes and let them "have their way"—until he reached a breaking point when they had "gone too far."

Joe began to attend individual sessions with me to work on what he referred to as his "anger problem with the kids." My first coaching of Joe began with a look back into his family of origin in order to try to understand how he had learned to do his "anger dance" with his children. It was reminiscent of my own family and set off my memories of a father out of control. Joe's childhood memories revealed that his father could also be calm and mild-mannered and yet extremely angry when his children stepped over some imaginary line. It was upsetting for Joe to look at how similar he was to his father and he was unwilling, at first, to consider my suggestion that he would benefit from approaching his father in new ways. I realized that Joe was not ready to work with his family of origin at that time, even though he had told me he didn't want to repeat old patterns of raging at his children.

The way Joe viewed his anger was a problem in itself. He saw his outbursts as "reflexive actions" that just came over him and were "out of his control." I explained to Joe that I was going to try to play the role of his coach and give him several assignments to work on in his family. He seemed to like this approach and responded positively to the challenge. Joe's first task was just to stay focused on himself while he spent time with his children. I felt that if Joe was able to take even a small step back to where he could observe his own reactions, he would become more aware of how his anger built.

Fathers are frequently lacking in self-focus as a skill. They are accustomed to observing what is going on around them, but not what is occurring within. For many men, the task of concentrated self-observation is new and unsettling, and the coach can be an important support in the process.

Joe returned to our next session with a more accurate picture of how his initial accommodation to his children's wishes could turn into a scene of rage later on. He was now able to see how his belief that he was being a "nice guy" by going along with his children's minor infractions led to blowups because he felt taken advantage of. I labeled Joe's compliant position as "Mr. Nice Guy," and later, we were both able to laugh together about how Mr. Nice Guy could turn into "Mr. Nasty" with very little warning.

No More "Mr. Nice Guy"

Joe's next assignment was to track the complete transformation of Mr. Nice Guy into Mr. Nasty, taking note of every change that occurred along the way. Joe was able to see how the nice guy within began to feel exploited, which allowed him to get angry and explode. This was the first time in his life that he saw himself as having a role in the anger that he produced, and not merely as the victim of the selfish acts of others.

In the next session, I asked Joe what it would be like for him to take an entirely different position by stopping Mr. Nice Guy in his tracks before he had the opportunity to turn nasty.

If Joe were able to think out a new position instead of simply reacting in old patterned ways, he would have moved to a higher level of self.

Joe and I worked together to plan a new way to manage his reactions to his children before he allowed them to "go too far."

He rehearsed what are known as "I messages" in which he would state clearly what the children could and could not do. He would bypass the feeling of being taken advantage of by sticking to his rules and backing them up calmly with a plan to take away something if his children refused to listen to him. I asked Joe to predict how his children might "test" his new way of handling things and how he might respond to their reactions.

At first, Joanne and Marcus were surprised when their father explained his new set of expectations. They did break the new rules several times to find out if Dad would enforce them as he'd promised. Joe stuck to his plan. He never lost his temper and seemed to gain a sense of his own power as his new strategies changed the dynamics of family life. He had spent most of his life blaming others for his own pain, but he was learning that *changing relationships is always about bringing more of a self-focus to whatever is going on.*

10

PROBLEM CHILDREN AND DISTANT DADS

M EN HAVE BEEN TRAINED to be aware of who is "in charge" of the various chores and responsibilities in the home, but problems can arise depending upon how those responsibilities are divided between fathers and mothers. If we see ourselves in charge of only the "bread and butter" issues while our wives are viewed as the sole proprietors of the children's lives, we may create problems down the road. We may feel that if there is a competent mother who is in total charge of the children we have discharged our obligation. In actuality, this kind of rigid division of family responsibility has not worked for most families.

Cheryl and Dick Thompson are a family whom I counseled. They were a concerned couple with a son who was out of control in the classroom. I viewed their child's behavior as a symptom of the father's absence from the family's daily life and I saw my primary goal as bringing the father back into the picture.

Any parent who has ever received a note or a call from school which said that their child was having problems knows how upsetting this can be. Nobody wants to believe that there is really anything wrong with his own son or daughter. Thus, our first reaction to a call from our child's school is often anger and disbelief. Sometimes the school is informing parents about a specific learning problem that can be dealt with by an evaluation and some remedial work, but often it is a behavior problem that does not respond to any simple remedy or easy solution. There is usually a "father factor" at work when children act up in school. The following story illustrates how parents can work cooperatively to resolve this kind of problem.

The School-Family Standoff

Cheryl's phone seemed to ring off the hook one afternoon in late October. Just when she had a few moments to sit down and collect her thoughts, the assistant principal, Mr. Adler, called to say that her eight-year-old son Greg had gotten into another fight and that he would like to meet with her the next morning. It was always the same thing with Greg. He "did not follow the rules in class" and was always "getting into fights during lunch." The last time Mrs. Thompson was asked to come to school occurred at the beginning of the school year. On that occasion, Mrs. Nathan, Greg's third grade teacher, told his mother that her son spent more time out of his seat than he did in it, and that he seemed to find it more important to impress his classmates with antics than to listen to his teachers.

Cheryl Thompson found herself growing impatient as she listened to Mr. Adler drone on about the latest incident involving her son. She picked up what she thought was criticism in his voice, and she tried hard not to become defensive. On one level she felt, "You're supposed to be professionals. Can't you control an eight-year-old?" But another part of her worried that Greg was gaining a school-wide reputation as a troublemaker. He was never difficult at home, and an evaluation by the school's child study team had determined that there were no deficits in his ability to master basic skills. Yet, the school had already begun to label Greg Thompson as a "problem child."

How does a problem like the one between the Thompson family and the school get resolved, and where does the problem lie? Did the problem exist inside of Greg since he was the one who displayed the negative behavior? Or did the key to understanding the problem reside in the school's inability to enforce its code of behavior? What about Greg's parents? Might they be the culprits because they were too lenient in the way that they set limits and imposed discipline at home?

The anxiety and uncertainty about who was responsible for Greg's behavior turned the morning meeting between Mrs. Thompson and Mr. Adler into a blame session with school and family more at odds than before they met. Mrs. Thompson felt that Mr. Adler was implying that she might not be doing enough to teach Greg a proper respect for authority, and began to defend her parenting. She wondered out loud about the competence of a staff that was unable to manage a third grader who was never disrespectful at home. However, when Mr. Adler asked what his mother wanted the school to do the next time Greg misbehaved, Mrs. Thompson didn't have an answer.

When parents and school administrators reach an impasse like this one, I as the school's social worker am sometimes called in to see if there are any unexplored options. I can usually offer a different perspective on where the problem is "located," and occasionally come up with a solution. By the time Mrs. Thompson arrived at my office following the meeting with the assistant principal, she was fed up with the school. She viewed me as another member of the enemy camp who saw her son as a "disruptive child" and was certain to criticize her parenting. I realized that my approach toward Mrs. Thompson would have to establish that I was capable of seeing things differently from the rest of the school administration if anything meaningful was to occur.

I reassured Mrs. Thompson that I was willing to look at how we might work together to solve this problem.

The Father Factor

After posing some initial questions to Mrs. Thompson about the method by which she'd attempted to deal with her son's school behavior problems, I learned that Greg's father was also living in this home, but had little to do with such matters. Mr. Thompson worked long hours at two jobs and even his weekends were sometimes taken up with overtime shifts. The dialogue between Mrs. Thompson and myself was a familiar one to me:

ME: I realize that Mr. Thompson works two jobs, but are you able to spend any time together? And when does he find the time to be with his children?

MRS. T.: John and I just don't get time alone these days. We used to before Janice was born when we had a regular baby-sitter. I know that the kids need to spend time with their father, but we also need both of his incomes to make ends meet. He's almost never home, and I end up taking care of Greg and Janice alone.

ME: How have you tried to handle the situation when you've gotten reports from the school of Greg's misbehavior?

MRS. T.: When I hear that he's been acting up, he always gets punished. Believe me, I've tried hitting him and taking away his Nintendo. The last time, he had early lights-out and no television for a week. He's okay for a day or two, but nothing really seems to work.

ME: Do you and Mr. Thompson agree about the way you've been disciplining Greg?

MRS. T.: We've never even gotten to talk about it.
Sometimes, I fill him in on what's been happening with
the kids, but I'm really the one in charge of everything.

Without ever having met Mr. Thompson, it was apparent
to me that there was a problem in this family, and not in relation
to Greg. There is a fertile ground for problems to grow when a
father is so removed from the lives of his children. The tensions
are compounded when very little is going on in the marriage. The
primary problem in the Thompson family was the lack of meaningful and intimate communication between the parents, but, as
in many dysfunctional families, the symptoms had turned up
somewhere else in the family. In this case, Greg's acting up in
school was the symptom.

*Symptoms in dysfunctional families signal that there is a
problem somewhere in the system, but they may also dis-
guise what is wrong at the same time. The child identified
as a "school behavior problem" often reflects a problem
between his parents. The distant outsider position of the
father in the family may fuel the intensity of what is acted
out in the classroom.*

Since Mr. Thompson seemed to be the missing link in his
family's problems, it became my goal to bring him into direct
contact with what was going on. I told Mrs. Thompson that I
believed that she had done the best she could with Greg under the
circumstances, but that her husband had to be included in whatever we decided to do next if we were going to help her son. Mrs.
Thompson said that it was going to be difficult to get her husband
to take time off from work, but I offered to meet with them early
in the morning so that he wouldn't have to lose a full day. She
still seemed hesitant, but I stated my position very clearly.

"I think that I can help," I said, "but I don't believe that I will be able to unless I can meet with Mr. Thompson one time."

At that point, Mrs. Thompson said that she would make sure that her husband came with her for our next meeting.

It is easier for helping professionals to simply go along with the system by seeing the child as the problem or only speaking with the mother because she is the more available parent. Neither the child nor the family benefits when this occurs.

When I insisted on including Mr. Thompson at a meeting about his son, I encroached on the way this family operated. He might have seen himself as being pulled away from where he was supposed to be. His wife might have viewed my demand as another attack on her role as primary caretaker of their children. I had to keep in mind, as a counselor and a coach, that change rarely comes about without conflict, and that I also had to be able to tolerate the anxiety that got stirred up by my interviews.

Highlighting a Father's Importance to His Family

Mr. Thompson came to my office early one morning with his wife. He didn't appear to be angry or unhappy about having to go to work late that day. He seemed mainly surprised and a little amused that I thought his input was important enough to insist that he be present, especially since he normally had so little to do with his children's lives.

My demand that a father be present at a meeting which concerned his children is also a statement that he is a necessary participant rather than a peripheral player in family matters.

I explained to Mr. and Mrs. Thompson that it was important that I get both of their ideas and opinions on how to solve this problem. First, however, I needed to understand how they each viewed what was going on with Greg. It became apparent that Mr. Thompson had always felt that his wife was not being strict enough with his son. Even so, he had stopped expressing his opinion, since he saw her as the one in charge. Even as we discussed this in our session, Mrs. Thompson stated that her husband just wasn't around the children enough to know the best way to handle a situation with them. Mr. Thompson seemed to withdraw as his wife reasserted her primary role as the "expert" on the children, but I felt that it was my responsibility to challenge this family pattern, since I saw it to be the core of their difficulties. I asked Mrs. Thompson, "What further information would your husband need on a regular basis in order to make sound decisions with you regarding your children?" As it turned out, both of them were receptive to the idea that Mr. Thompson needed to know what was going on in his home, even if it meant that Mrs. Thompson would initially just tell him about his children's day when he came home too late to speak with them in person. Their second "assignment," which involved the need for a higher level of cooperation, opened up the possibility that further conflict would develop.

I said, "I'd like you to create a plan together for how you might deal with Gregory's behavior in school."

This task challenged the way roles were divided between these parents and asked them to relate as equals in this arena. If they were able to take this on, it would also force them to look at some of their differences, and, if they were able to deal with their differences, their parenting and marriage had the potential to grow. I discussed with them and gave them a copy of a basic guideline on effective discipline with children. Then I asked if they could continue their dialogue during the week. If they were able to begin a negotiation on their own, then it would bode well for continued work toward resolving other problems in the family.

There is no "right way" to overcome discipline problems with children that works for every family. All families are unique and parents usually carry differing rules and roles from their own families of origin. The guideline that I offered the Thompsons is one that has had a particular appeal to the fathers with whom I have worked because it is a practical and measurable approach to change.

Effective Discipline Techniques for Parents: Some Guidelines

1. Effective discipline is created by plan, not on impulse.
2. In order for any plan to work, there must be agreement and ongoing communication between the adults involved.
3. Effective discipline must be consistent in the way that it is implemented and reinforced.
4. In order for discipline measures to be effective, they must make sense to your child and be appropriate to his or her age.
5. Effective discipline involves calm and thoughtful communication. Discipline loses its power if it goes on in the heat of anger or during a family scene.
6. Any discipline plan should be monitored to see whether or not it is bringing about the intended change in behavior.
7. Children should be involved in thinking and making decisions about their choices and its consequences within the plan.
8. The consequences or "punishments" that may involve the children should not punish or inconvenience the parents.
9. Rewards are often more effective than taking privileges

away from a child. If both are used, they should be kept separate. Something that is earned should never be taken away for a later infraction.

10. Effective discipline involves careful evaluation and innovation when needed. Those measures that are not working should be reconsidered by the involved parties.

Following Through

The Thompsons came to see me three more times. They were able to create a plan by which Greg would receive rewards for positive behaviors, and lose specific privileges if he did not abide by the rules at school or at home. The plan itself was similar to what Mrs. Thompson had been doing on her own. The difference was the increased participation of her husband and his commitment to its enforcement. At our second meeting, I reviewed the Thompsons' plan and they rehearsed how they would present it to Greg. I made it clear that it was crucial for them to both approach Greg so he would see that mother and father had come up with this plan together. I explained that I had counseled children who secretly believed that the less vocal parent was "on their side" until they finally saw both of their parents supporting each other's positions.

The Thompsons had decided that they wanted to present their new code of rules and expectations to Greg in my office with my participation. I agreed, since it reinforced the idea that the school was included as part of the new plan. Greg was called out of his class. He was shocked to see his father in my office. I imagine that this was the first time Greg had seen his father inside of his school. He felt both a sense of importance to warrant such a visit, and a little intimidated by his father's presence.

Mr. and Mrs. Thompson did a fine job of communicating their new code of behavior to Greg and they made sure to support each other's comments and assertions. Greg was very quiet and respectful throughout the discussion. I called his mother and father out of my office and asked if they would consider meeting for five minutes with Mrs. Nathan, Greg's teacher. I told them that this would make it even clearer to Greg that we were all working together on this plan, and that he would be less inclined to act out in school.

The brief meeting in the hallway outside of his class was probably an important one in the life of Greg Thompson. Three important figures in his life met together to determine how they were going to deal with his bad behavior. And this all happened within a half hour of Greg finding his father in his school presenting Greg with a new set of rules in solid agreement with his mother. As Greg stood in that small circle with his parents, his teacher and me, he heard Mrs. Nathan say that she would call the Thompsons if there were any further problems in school, and Greg saw his father give her his work number.

My third and final meeting with the Thompsons was a happier one. They were pleased that a week had gone by without incident and thanked me for my advice. The tone of the meeting was lighter and I was able to joke with them in a serious vein.

"So," I said, "I know that you're still working double overtime, Mr. Thompson, but when was the last time the two of you had a date together?"

There were two things that would throw the Thompson family off-course, and both of them had to do with Mr. Thompson's role as the breadwinner and his limited time at home. If Mr. and Mrs. Thompson continued a dialogue about their children but spent no time away from their children, their marriage would eventually grow flat and lifeless. The distance and underlying tensions of that type of marriage always take a toll on the children. If Mr. Thompson were to continue to be an equal partner when it came to discipline but had no special time to set aside for his son, there was a strong possibility that problems with Greg would resurface at some point. Mr. and Mrs. Thompson said that conversations about Greg and his problems had renewed some communication in their marriage, but that they would have to work at finding a baby-sitter and finding time alone as husband and wife. I was less sure that Mr. Thompson was committed to spending time alone with his son.

I asked Mr. Thompson if he could stay for a few minutes after his wife left and before he went to work. I wanted to leave him with the idea that the time he spent with his son was vital for both of them.

I told Mr. Thompson that I was also a father and that, like him, I worked long hours and late evenings. I said that when I had time away from work, I felt pulled in different directions as he did. I shared with him my lack of fathering from my own past and how we, as men, needed to figure out ways of not making our fathers' mistakes with our own kids. When I was finished speaking, I could see that I had reached him in a positive way.

The dialogue that I have with men about fatherhood has much more to do with coaching than what is usually called "therapy." As a coach I may be an expert, but in a conversation with another father I prefer to speak also as a father. Then we are two men playing on the same team. The role of the therapist, as professional and expert, is what I believe has turned many men away from seeking help. I have done my best work with men when I step out of the therapist's persona and speak to them as one father to another.

Are We Encouraging Fathers to Participate in the Family Dialogue?

The following is a checklist for teachers, guidance counselors, social workers, psychologists, and other members of the helping professions.

1. If a mother tells you that her husband has to work and cannot attend a meeting or conference that concerns his child, do you ever try to make a special arrangement to accommodate his work schedule? Have you ever pressed the issue by emphasizing the importance of having at least one meeting with both parents present so that you can at least meet the father?

2. When a father attends a meeting about his child, he may defer to his wife's "expertise" by saying very little. Do you make sure to encourage his participation by getting his opinion, too?

3. Professionals have been trained to remain neutral and objective about the problems that are presented, but that often works to maintain the status quo. Have you ever taken a position with parents when you see that the roles are divided in such a way that a father has almost nothing to do with his children?

4. When dealing with a separated family, do you include the non-custodial parent in all meetings and make sure that he is equally informed about what is going on with his child?

11

RITES OF PASSAGE

Fathers and Teenagers

OF ALL THE PHASES that a family will go through, raising teenage children can provide the greatest challenge. Adolescents are "peer groupers" who often bring new behaviors, ideas, and people into the home. Some of this self-expression is bound to clash with the behavior patterns parents have set up and desire. Fathers, in particular, can be drawn into conflicts with teenagers when they view the adolescents as a threat to their own authority and control. For the adolescent, the issue of control also arises as he or she struggles under the impact of sensations and impulses that he barely understands.

The passage through this tumultuous period involves the "task" of creating a distinct self—what philosopher and psychologist Erik Erikson has referred to as the formation of an identity. On the negative side of the developmental ledger is what he termed "role confusion," in which the developing self forms around a core of self-destructive or antisocial behaviors.

As a society we tend to think of *individuals going through phases in their lives.* We are less inclined to view the *entire family*—not just a collection of individuals but an emotional unit with its own patterned ways of doing things over many generations—as passing from one cycle to the next. However, if we could conceptualize in this way, we would see a teenager move towards separation within the unique emotional system that is his family. The family, in turn, would be viewed as an "organism" that also adapts and modifies its responses in reaction to the stresses of adolescent development.

What has been and should be the role of fathers during this phase of the family life cycle? Although, in many cases, the father has been the "second parent" and primarily the family breadwinner while his children were young, there sometimes emerges an expectation that he will play a more influential role when his children reach adolescence.

If juvenile delinquency is in part the result of under involved fathers, then how will the adolescent son be welcomed into the world of men? The image of the pre-industrial father making miracles out of raw leather or iron with his son at his side may be a romantic one, but it is the one that implies physical presence.

When a father in our culture tries to become an important force in his adolescent son's life during his adolescence but has not taken the time to be there in all of the seasons of the boy's growing up, the father will run into difficulties. He may find himself in the role of the enforcer of limits without a firm basis for his wish to be in control.

The Controlling Father

Much of this book has been devoted to understanding the underfunctioning father. One the other end of the spectrum is the parent who expects to be involved in all aspects of his children's life, but has an unrealistic need to have things *his* way.

Sylvia Cary, a Los Angeles-based psychotherapist and author, sees the controlling father as a "man who always has to run the show." He thinks he knows best how things should turn out and how his children must behave. Frank Pittman takes a lighter look at this serious problem in his book entitled, *Man Enough*:

> Men have felt called upon by good authority to control things. In our blessed little heads, we have felt a divine responsibility to conquer and control nature, to conquer and control men who are in some way different from ourselves, and, of course, to conquer women, who otherwise would surely go out of control and create disturbances and disorder.
> Dominion over people and things had passed on from God to Adam to Dad to us.

Fathers in good control are task-oriented and able to direct the creative energy of their children. According to Cary, fathers who are "bad" controllers manipulate their children through overprotection, insults, lectures, bribes, and criticism. Many of these men grew up in out of control families and, thus, they have resolved on some level that they would never allow things to get out of control again. The family drama intensifies when the child of the overcontrolling father becomes an adolescent. This occurs, in part, because a teenager may overfunction on one day and underfunction on the next. A father who is predisposed to fixing things and people may feel compelled to step in and "get things working right."

For the teenager who may need to experiment with new behaviors, the controlling father may become the catalyst to the feared rebelliousness. This turned out to be the case with Joseph, a New York City police officer who brought his fifteen-year-old son to see me because, "Ken is completely out of control."

Breaking the Family Control-Rebellion Cycle

When I saw Ken for our initial session, he described a life in which he had shuttled back and forth between his parents' homes since their divorce when he was three. Beginning at age seven, Ken's elementary school years were spent mostly with his mother and her live-in boyfriend, John. Ken related that he felt mistreated by John, but he was unable to offer specific examples of abuse or neglect. When Ken discussed his father, I was struck by how infrequently Ken had seen his father during this period— a classic case of a father and child losing contact after a divorce. It had been a very difficult time for Ken. At the same time that he virtually lost his father, he had been uprooted from his neighborhood and thrust into a new household with his mother and her boyfriend. It became clear to me that John viewed Ken as an appendage in a family life that he could have done without. In addition to missing his old home, Ken had become the new kid on the block and the target of the local bullies. Abandoned by the most important man in his life, Ken evolved into an angry street fighter with a reputation for hurting any kid who dared to get in his way.

As Ken told me about his prowess as a fighter, I could see that this was a source of pride and power in a world in which he had always felt weak and unprotected.

At age fourteen-and-a-half, Ken had returned to living with his father in his father's apartment in the Bronx. His mother had finally thrown up her hands after a valiant effort trying to enforce her household rules with little support from Ken's father. At that point, Ken was cutting out of high school regularly and throwing parties at his mother's apartment when she was at work. When they had been married, she had always relied upon Ken's father to "lay down the law." Now she was handing Ken back to him to set the limits that she could no longer enforce.

When Joseph brought Ken to see me, the dysfunctional pattern of behavior between them had reached a crescendo. The more the father tried to control his son's behavior with punishments, the more Ken found ways of breaking other rules when his father wasn't looking. Finally, Ken was caught stealing spray paint cans from a hardware store in the Bronx. He had been painting graffiti in the subway repair yards, dodging watchmen and German shepherds.

Joseph used Marine Corps techniques—cleanups and forced exercise routines—as his son's punishments, but Ken's destructive behavior pattern was escalating as more dangerous and illegal acts followed each disciplinary measure that his father meted out. There was little real communication between father and son. Instead, it seemed to me, a ritualized "conversation" was being acted out.

In his mind, the father was saying: I'll show you what happens when you challenge my authority and break the law that I represent.

And his son was replying, You can't stop me from doing what I want to, no matter how much you try to control me.

It was clear to me that a system had been created in which one family member's behavior set off a predictable response in another member. Consequently, the second behavior reinforced the original behavior which it had been intended to change.

A vicious circle had been created, in which the very behavior the parent used to resolve the problem was actually making it worse.

I soon perceived that Ken was not going to budge in his rebellious stance, propelled by the force of his need to individuate and to show that he could not be controlled. If change was going to occur, it had to come from Ken's father being able to adopt a new position relative to his son.

In my second meeting with Joseph, I presented him with a diagram of the destructive cycle that I saw going on between him and Ken. It looked something like this:

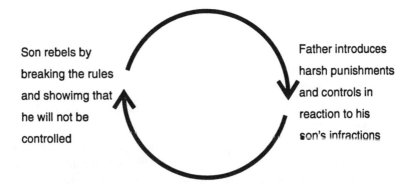

Son rebels by breaking the rules and showimg that he will not be controlled

Father introduces harsh punishments and controls in reaction to his son's infractions

The diagram was my attempt to graphically illustrate a pattern that could only be changed if the father became objective enough to see his own participation. It required a calmer, more differentiated position than he had been able to demonstrate up to this point.

My coaching of Ken's father involved coaxing him to experiment with a different response to his son's behaviors:

COACH: This diagram is my way of showing a pattern that is going on—but not changing. Right now, it's a kind of vicious circle. You punish and he disobeys. He disobeys and you punish . . . and so on.

FATHER: That is what's happening but I still feel that I'm doing the right thing. I'm his father. He's breaking the law, and I'm setting the punishments.

COACH: But are the punishments working?

FATHER: (After a pause.) They should be working, but I guess they're not. I was thinking about sending Ken away.

COACH: Before you do, would you be willing to try

something different?

FATHER: Just about anything right now.

COACH: When Ken breaks a rule or gets into trouble the next time, would you be willing to try something new?

FATHER: What would you like me to do?

COACH: Were there any things that you can remember that you and Ken enjoyed doing together when he was younger?

FATHER: We used to go to Yankee games together at the stadium. Are you saying that I should reward him by taking him to a ball game when he does something wrong?

COACH: I'm saying that your punishments aren't working and it may be time to try a new approach. I was thinking that getting out of the house and doing something together would give you and him an opportunity to talk.

FATHER: I almost don't know what to say to him anymore.

COACH: I know. Why don't you start by admitting that this whole system of punishments and rebellion has not been working. He knows it and so do you.

FATHER: I feel like I'd be tying my hands. I need to be able to punish Ken when he misbehaves.

COACH: I don't think you have to give up your right to set limits. I just think you both need to figure out a new way of relating to each other that respects that Ken is almost an adult and that you've also moved on in your life since he was a little kid whom you could punish without question.

Not long after we had begun our coaching sessions, Ken and Joseph went to a Yankee game. Ken was suspicious at first, but seemed to appreciate the fact that his father was able to admit that the punishments weren't working. When Ken saw me two weeks later, he seemed calmer. He told me that he felt that "the pressure was off" at home. I took that to mean that he no longer had to prove that he could not be controlled by his father's punishments and was now free to move on to more constructive pursuits.

The Godfather

I have previously noted how a father will often have a powerful impact on his children, even though he may seem to be the less involved parent. This turned out to be the case with seventeen-year-old Penny who had dropped out of school, refused to work, and spent most of her time behind closed doors.

Penny and her parents were clients of Peggy Papp, a family therapist known for her pioneering work in the field. On the surface, this family might have appeared to be a "classic case" of an over involved mother who was having trouble "letting go" of her youngest child. The child's symptoms have traditionally been viewed by therapists as a reflection of the "neurotic mother's need to hold on." However, Ms. Papp knew that mother's "over involvement" has been the focus of generations of therapists who have tried to pry mother and child apart while ignoring the significant role that fathers play in what is going on.

When we exclusively focus on mothers as the root of their children's problems, we are at the same time negating the importance of fathers.

The following are some of Ms. Papp's descriptions and dialogue as she worked with Penny's family and helped them to see the role of her father's controlling behavior in the problems that they were presenting:

Penny was the youngest of five children and the only one presently living at home. She reluctantly accompanied her parents to therapy, where she participated minimally, responding to questions with shrugs or monosyllables. Mother spoke in quiet desperation and implored us to help her daughter. She gave a detailed description of Penny's gradual withdrawal from family and friends, her dropping out of school, her erratic moods, and seclusion in her room. Father, a huge, impressive-looking man with a hearty personality, expressed his concern about both his daughter and his wife. "Her whole being is consumed with worry about Penny," he said. "She watches Penny's every move, and talks about nothing else day and night." He had suggested his wife go to individual therapy, but mother insisted they come as a family.

Although father complained about mother worrying too much, he also conceded that his wife's preoccupation with his daughter also reassured him. "Worry is also taking care of," he said. "If I know she is worried about Penny, I know Penny is going to be taken care of." When the therapist said that this let him off the hook, he laughed and replied, "You're damned right. I planned it that way, too. If I didn't have my wife, I'd go crazy."

What was his wife's view of all this? "It's not fair," she said. "It makes me angry. Why should I have to do all the worrying? She's 'our' daughter, not 'my' daughter." Father dismissed his wife's worrying as a personal problem, saying if she didn't have something to worry about, she would manufacture it because she was a born "worrier."

Mother denied she needed to worry. She insisted it would be a big relief to her if she could stop worrying, but she complained that whenever she tried to discuss her concerns with her husband, rather than listening and understanding, he either cut her off saying, "I don't want to hear anymore," or felt compelled to take action on his own and "fix" the situation. This usually involved charging into Penny's room and laying down the law to her. When she defied him, he flew into a rage and threatened violence. Mother then interceded to protect both of them.

All messages between Penny and father went through mother, who acted as the mediator and tried to keep peace between them. Mother said, "I go back and forth between Penny and my husband. I don't think that's good. They should have their own communication, but I'm afraid someone will get hurt."

At one important juncture in the counseling of this family, Penny's father admitted that he did not want his teenage daughter to grow up. His disclosure led to the following exchange :

THERAPIST: How young do you want Penny to stay?

FATHER: About eight. No, really, I'm just kidding. But, that's what I miss. I want to give others everything and make them happy, buy them things and take care of them. She doesn't respond to that anymore, and I don't know what else to do.

MOTHER: He's a giver, but he can't receive. There's nothing he will let me do for him. He likes to become completely independent—which in a way is wonderful. I never have to pick up his socks, take things to the cleaners and it's always, "Let's go out for dinner so you won't have to cook."

FATHER: I can't stand anyone doing anything for me. If it's my birthday, I want to give you a present.

MOTHER: It makes others feel not appreciated, not needed.

THERAPIST: (To mother.) So you feel deprived when your husband doesn't let you get him anything?

MOTHER: Yes, when he has a cold, he won't let me take care of him. On Father's Day, he won't even open his presents.

THERAPIST: (To father.) Do you deprive everyone in the family in this way?

MOTHER: Yes, deprive, that's the word.

THERAPIST. (To Penny.) Penny, does your father let you do anything for him?

PENNY: (Shrugging her shoulders.) I don't care.

MOTHER: The way I see it is you're doing others a favor by allowing them to do things for you. Independence is a great thing, but there is another word—interdependence—that I think is better. I see this as his being one up. He's like this with friends and in business.

FATHER: Very true. Every time I take one, I want to give you three.

MOTHER: I see it as one-upmanship.

THERAPIST: (To father.) You feel it's better to have others obligated to you rather than you obligated to them?

FATHER: Yes, I can't stand to feel obligated. If I do a favor for someone, I don't ever want them to pay me back. I was watching *The Godfather* the other night and I said, "I'd like to be the Godfather."

MOTHER: And I said, "You are. You don't know it."

FATHER: And she's right. I can't call in my favors. That's my problem. I have to pick up the check all the time.

MOTHER: (To father.) I feel sorry for you that you can't get more pleasure out of the things being done for you. It keeps people from getting close to you.

FATHER: If I get too close I have to worry about you—you become a responsibility. When someone gets close to me, I start backing off.

THERAPIST: And how does that work between you and your wife?

FATHER: I don't know if there's a relation with that. I know when I'm sick I don't want her to take care of me. I don't want to feel weak. If she takes care of me too much, I am weak. I don't want others to take care of me. I'll take care of them.

Relinquishing Control by Learning to Receive

This father's image of himself as "The Godfather" is an example of emulating the male cultural hero—powerful, paternal, independent, self-possessed and emotionally detached.

He was only comfortable when he was in control of relationships, which to him meant never needing anyone and having others beholden to him. The way he kept others beholden to him was through a common male power play showering family, friends, and business associates with gifts and favors.

When his daughter became a teenager and he could no longer function as provider, protector, and playmate to his "little girl," he distanced himself, and left all the daily worrying and caretaking up to mother. Mother, following the dictates of what she considered to be her maternal responsibility, automatically accepted this job. Father then blamed the daughter's problems on mother's "overinvolvement," unaware of the connection between her "overinvolvement" and his distant relationship with both mother and daughter.

Ms. Papp's coaching of this family involved helping Penny's father experience a personal relationship that involved receiving as well as giving. She instructed him as follows:

At least twice a week, father was to ask Penny to do something for him and allow her to do it. It could be anything except something that involved her welfare, such as going back to school, getting a job, leaving her room, etc. It must be something that involved his well-being and he must thank her for it. Penny was asked to comply with his request and that way teach him how to receive.

By reversing the positions of giver and receiver, Penny was taken out of her little-girl position and treated like a competent adult who had something valuable to teach her father. By having to ask and receive, father was compelled to relinquish his Godfather position and become involved in the give-and-take of a more equal relationship.

For the first time since the therapy began, Penny came alive.

She raised her head and joined her parents in laughter at the thought of her father receiving anything. She doubted that he would be able to do the assignment, saying, "I can't imagine anyone teaching him anything. He knows it all."

Father was surprised by the turning of the tables and agreed it would be difficult. But, true to form, he declared, "It will kill me, but I'll die trying." Mother looked relieved.

Father made two requests of Penny, with great difficulty: one, that she go to the corner drug store and buy him the Sunday newspaper, and two, that she get him a book that he needed from the library. Both of these activities got Penny out of her room and put the father/daughter relationship on a different footing. As father began to move out of his Godfather position, the distance between them was reduced, permitting a more open and honest exchange. Mother became less worried as Penny showed signs of becoming more communicative and began leaving her room. She was no longer compelled to mediate between Penny and her father and felt a great burden had been lifted.

Within a few weeks, Penny had a job and didn't want to attend the sessions any more because she was too busy. Father's first reaction was to get furious and yell at mother because she was the one who set up the therapy. Why should he be willing to go and expose his head if Penny wasn't willing to expose hers? Penny became very upset over her parents' argument and retired to her room. This time, father broke the old cycle by doing something different. He went to Penny's room without mother's prompting and said, "Penny, I'm wrong. I'm learning, too, and that's why I'm coming to talk to you. I took it out on your mom and I didn't mean to. I'm really angry at you. So that's why I'm coming here with what I've got to complain about." They had a long discussion during which they argued with each other, became angry, cried, and finally reconciled. During the course of this intense exchange, Penny convinced her father that she was old enough to make up her own mind whether or not she wanted to continue coming to therapy.

A simple task had shifted the balance of power between the father and the daughter by reversing their positions of giver and receiver. But an even more significant shift was taking place through the field of therapy—away from an exclusive focus on the mother-child relationship, and toward the inclusion of the father as a significant participant in the family's emotional life.

One exercise that has proved effective with fathers who become aware they are being too controlling with their children is this:

Think of something that your child is really good at but that you know little about. Have your child teach you how to do that activity or task.

Relating to a child's competence is especially important if he or she is not functioning well in other areas and you tend to move in and "fix" things too quickly.

12

SECOND CHANCES

FATHER LOSS IS NOT only about the losses that children suffer when they miss out on fathering; it is also about the negative impact that not playing the role of the father can have on men's emotional development and mental health. Our missed opportunities to be involved fathers are often tied to an over-focus on career goals and breadwinning as young men. New circumstances and changing life cycle needs may give us a different perspective on the importance of our relationships with our children during our mid-life.

Divorce, the death of a spouse, or remarriage to a woman who has children from a former relationship may jar a man into taking another look at the role he has played in the life of his own children and others. These life events may make a man aware he wants to be a different kind of father than he may have been earlier.

For many men, divorce is no longer the final chapter in an unsuccessful family life. Diminished contact with their children may be a fact of life for many post-divorce fathers. For others, divorce is only a brief period in relationship histories that will include remarriage and participation in new families.

For some fathers in our era their family time line may look like this:

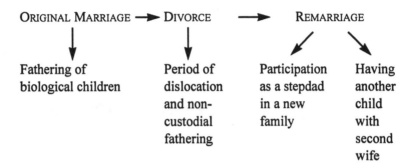

ORIGINAL MARRIAGE ➡ DIVORCE ➡ REMARRIAGE

| Fathering of biological children | Period of dislocation and non-custodial fathering | Participation as a stepdad in a new family | Having another child with second wife |

Many fathers I have counseled who are involved in new marriages and "blended families" learn and practice wisdom, patience, and a knowledge about relationships that they did not have in their first marriages and families. They usually seem more committed to making things work and are aware that they must also make a strong effort if their new household is going to mesh.

Fathers and Divorce

There are two elements that determine how a child will cope with the trauma of his parents' separation and divorce. The first element has to do with the custodial parent who is often, but not always, the mother. If that person can continue to parent and function well enough to manage a household in the face of the emotional and material losses that accompany divorce, then the child can identify with his parent's competence and survive the crisis. The second element has to do with the non-custodial parent—usually but not always the father—who has moved out of the home. Is the non-custodial parent able to maintain an ongoing connection and regular contact with his children throughout the separation and over the years following the divorce? In order to do this, a father must see himself as a fathering figure with a distinct identity as a parent. If the father sees his family as a "package" with mother and children fused together gratifying their needs against him, then the chances of sustaining father-child contact and satisfying his own needs following separation are extremely slim.

The emotional health and survival of a child from a divorcing family is linked to his father's capacity to separate his role as father from the feelings that he may harbor toward his ex-wife and the defunct marriage.

One of the more damaging aspects of marital separation for the child is the potential for him or her to "absorb" the unresolved emotional intensity left over from the marriage. The child runs the risk of becoming the "messenger" between the two ex-spouses. The degree to which basic communication has broken down between the two households is directly correlated to the degree to which the child from the separated family is being placed at risk.

The Losses of the Father

It may seem incredibly irresponsible to someone who has never been through a divorce for a parent not to place his children's well-being above his own emotional reactions to his ex-spouse. "Doesn't the father realize that his marriage may be over, but he is a parent for life?" is a question often asked by outsiders.

Yet, there are circumstances that can make it extremely difficult for a non-custodial divorced father to sustain a relationship with his children.

A visiting father who may only see his children on week-ends has lost the day-to-day contact that he may once have had. In his book *Fatherless America*, David Blankenhorn comments as follows:

> The Visiting Father is hard to see. He is a displaced man trying not to be the ex-father. The Visiting Father is one who has left the premises; he still stops by but he doesn't stay. He is on the outside looking in. He is a father once removed. This type of father cannot raise his children, he can only visit them. As these men move away from their former homes and drift away from their former wives, they also lose the essence of their father-hood. Even though they have the best intentions of not divorcing their children, they inevitable disconnect from them.

There is a popularly held notion that, unlike a woman, a man does not "need" the daily interactions with his children. It is often not understood that fathers end up cutting off from the pain of not being able to be with their children on a daily basis.

As a society, we may need to reexamine the way we view losses that result from divorce. We universally sympathize with the child who loses his father while we tend to ignore the impact of the loss of daily contact on the father who is losing the experience of raising his child.

The rituals of putting a child to bed or even sitting together in front of a television set can be a significant part of a father's emotional life. The fact that men are often less aware of their emotional needs and their grief does not serve to make the impact of the loss of daily contact with their children any less intense.

An added impediment to post-divorce father involvement is the father's feeling that the entire system is unfair and stacked against him. The fact that visitation is often tied to child support payments is almost always a source of conflict and resentment. Furthermore, the inequities of a legal system that has favored women in child custody cases can create a "What's the use?" attitude in men who might otherwise have remained more involved with their children. Jerold Lee Shapiro in his book on fatherhood, *The Measure of a Man*, characterizes the injustices against fathers in the following statement:

> In today's divorce court some women are treated as if they belong to a protected group, and their husbands as if they were the perpetrators of an injustice without any evidence to support that assumption. . . . The sum of these psychological, financial, and social problems faced by the non-custodial single fathers no doubt contributes greatly to these fathers' gradual withdrawal from the lives of their children. Fathering relationships do not seem to weather such obstacles and therefore tend to attenuate over time.

Divorced Fathers and the Need for Social Support

There should be a manual for divorcing fathers that explains what these men can expect to encounter and what type of help is available for them. If there were such a guide, it would probably include the following items:

1. A listing of Fathers' Rights organizations (See the Appendix.)

2. A guide on how to build a network of social support.

The most important survival skill for a divorcing father to have is a capacity to create a network of people whom he can turn to for practical help and emotional support.

It has been well documented that the mothers and fathers who fare the best following their separations are the ones who have superior support systems. Men who have always equated their masculinity with their ability to "go it alone" are most prone to depression and breakdown during this highly stressful period. Men often have fewer people to call upon than their wives, who usually have a group of women friends that they can turn to for help and emotional support.

Mothers without careers are often left with a lower standard of living after a separation, while fathers are usually left socially impoverished. Just as women have traditionally depended upon their husbands to be the breadwinners, men have relied upon their wives to provide them with a social life and emotional connections to others. As the material items are being divided up, divorced husbands are likely to discover that the couples they had socialized with are really his wife's friends, and he may be left isolated with little social support.

In order to find a system of social support, the divorcing father needs to either create or reconnect with the following networks:

1. THE FAMILY OF ORIGIN is a "natural" supportive network. Whether or not a family is seen as "supportive," a father will benefit from remaining connected to or reestablishing ties with relatives. Parents and other members of the extended family help to create a sense of sameness for children who may be feeling destabilized by the separation.

2. JOINING A SUPPORT GROUP has been necessary for survival for many fathers who are going through a divorce. The group experience is qualitatively different from individual counseling or coaching, which may also be helpful. It gives the father the opportunity to be open in front of others and to experience the advice and concern that he may not be receiving elsewhere. Groups have helped fathers avoid

contaminating their parenting with their anger toward their
ex-wives, and have made the periods when they are apart
from their children more bearable. The common pattern in
which a man gets involved with someone new before he has
really grieved the loss of his marriage can be averted by
participation in a support group.

(The appendices in the back of this book have further
information on forming groups and on resources for divorced
fathers.)

Being a Stepfather: Some Things to Consider

Stepfathering can be an opportunity for a man to become
a positive father figure to a child if he is able to balance his
authority with some restraint. When a man marries a woman who
has children from a prior relationship, he is joining a preexisting
family that has its own history, "culture," and ways of getting
things done. The younger the children when a stepdad arrives on
the scene, the greater the probability that they will view him as
their father.

A stepfather joins what is called a "blended family." This
is a family unit that may also include his children from a former
marriage. Trying to become a part of an already formed family is
like walking in on the middle of a movie. You know little about
the characters and almost nothing about the plot. The following
suggestions come out of my work with men who have struggled
with this very complicated role.

• When you become a member of a stepfamily, you are joining an organization that has been in existence long before
you came on the scene. Go slowly, respect differences and
observe how this new system operates before deciding to

make any important moves. The advantage of not having been a part of what has gone on over the years is that you may be able to offer some fresh perspective to your partner on what you see going on. You will be effective in this way only if you do not try to take over.

- Do not fall into the trap of trying to replace a father who is no longer in the home. The children should also be encouraged to see their father when possible. *The establishment of a positive relationship between you and your stepchildren may be contingent upon whether or not they are able to maintain an ongoing connection with their father. A cutoff between children and their father will produce a negative emotional fallout for everyone involved.*

- *Do not attempt to be the primary parent or the disciplinarian.* Since we have been trained as men to "fix" things and to protect the women in our life, we may be inclined to take charge in a new household as soon as we move in. Since women have also been trained to cede authority to men, they may see a new husband as the "rescuer," while another part of them may resent the intrusion. The most common complaint told to me by remarried fathers is that their new wives are too lenient and allow their children to get away with too much. They often feel personally challenged to take a stand on behavior that they perceive as disrespectful to their wives. *Taking on the role of disciplinarian is a formula for disaster for most stepfathers. It sets up a challenge and possible confrontation since the lines of authority are clearest between a natural parent and her children.* A predictable crisis that occurs when a stepfather oversteps his authority is one statement that is usually made by an adolescent: "I don't have to listen to you. You're not my father."

- The adolescent's challenge to the stepfather highlights the central question facing a man living in a blended family: *Can I be an important adult figure in this household without overstepping my wife's authority with her children?*

This is obviously not a question with a simple answer, but some stepfathers have been able to draw a line between mutually enforceable "household rules" and the specific discipline that a mother employs with her own children. I have found that a stepfather will almost always be more effective as an advisor and consultant to his wife than the dean of discipline to her children.

• *Adjust your expectations about the way you feel others should react to your joining the stepfamily.* It is important to keep in mind that the new marriage is not going to have a courtship or romantic period free from the emotional pulls, jealousies, and needs of your wife's children. Your stepchildren have already survived their parents' separation and may realistically see you as drawing their mother's attention away from them. *Expect the period of adjustment to take place over several years.*

Singe Parent Fathering

A common complaint that I hear in my discussions with fathers functioning as stepparents is that they're trying to be more involved parents, but their wives do not like their husband's way of handling the children. The things that may seem important to Mom may not matter as much to Dad. The question of who gets to decide the "right way" to handle the children has brought many couples into my office seeking help. I tell them first that there is, of course, no absolute "right way" to do anything. Couples must learn to negotiate each new situation as it arises. However, if stepfathers are going to be equal partners, then it must be realized that they will bring new ways of doing things into the mix. This is an important compromise, because, much as a woman might want her husband's participation as a parent, she may also see him as second in command when it comes to her children. Conflict is bound to arise when a father asserts his right to do things his way when he is alone with his children.

The single father will get the opportunity to do things entirely his way, but he will also begin to experience the exhaustion, worry, and occasional exhilaration that mothers have dealt with for generations. A single mother is a cultural norm that we have come to accept, but fathering is still not thought of as a task that men are able to do by themselves. New statistics tell otherwise. As of 1990, 890,000 single parent fathers had custody of more than one million children. Although this represents only one-sixth of the single parent households headed by women, there are clearly a significant number of fathers who are parenting their children by themselves.

In his book *The Nurturing Father*, Kyle Pruett has contributed to our knowledge by interviewing many fathers who have taken on the role of primary parent in their families. He leaves little question about the capacity of fathers to provide an emotional climate in which children can thrive. On the other hand, there are important obstacles to good parenting that single fathers need to overcome that are a result of our male conditioning:

- While mothers generally have no doubt that they are in charge of their children's lives, men have not been trained to place their children first.

- Fathers are often unaware of the myriad of details that are a part of the day-to-day lives of their children. It can be a revelation when we realize that this is a full-time job.

- Fathers may lack some of the basic household skills such as budgeting, cooking, and shopping.

• We are not a part of the carpooling and mutual favor networks that have made the lives of mothers more manageable.

The relationship between a single father and his children will depend on what one author has described as learning to be an "Earth Father," as opposed to a "Sky Father." Whereas the Sky Father is an emotionally distant provider, the Earth Father has learned how to be nurturing and emotionally accessible. He knows that he has to remember about snacks and play dates, and he is able to put away his newspaper to play with his children.

The single father is usually dealing with the loss of his spouse and his marriage while, at the same time, he is adjusting to his new caretaker role. More than 200,000 single fathers are widowers whose bond with their children is also tied to the death of the single most important person in each of their lives. Both father and child have suffered wounds whose healing largely depends upon the quality of communication between them.

The phases of loss and renewal following the loss of a mother from a household are well illustrated in the 1979 movie, *Kramer vs. Kramer*. Dustin Hoffman's character, Ted Kramer, is climbing the corporate ladder when his wife, played by Meryl Streep, decides that her role as homemaker is just too constricting for her at this point in her life. She departs suddenly, leaving the household and the care of their six-year-old son Billy entirely to her husband. Kramer is left without a marriage, and he is also left in charge of the son that he has been too busy to get to know.

Billy has literally been dropped into Ted Kramer's lap, and the audience is able to watch as Ted tries to juggle his career demands against the daily needs of his son.

Both father and son are in a state of shock on the morning following Mrs. Kramer's leaving, and the tension is palpable as they try to make breakfast together.

Mr. Kramer attempts to keep things light, but his underlying resentment erupts along with the frying pan and his coffee, which both end up on the kitchen floor. What he is not ready to face at this point is the sadness and grief that accompany the end of his marriage.

In a later scene, Billy defies his father who has directed him to let go of a container of ice cream. Kramer is tired of being tested by his son, and he grabs Billy, who is kicking and screaming, and places him in his bedroom with the light off. We can say at this point that father has descended from the sky and landed solidly on mother earth. Later that evening, father and son have their first important dialogue, and Kramer demonstrates that he can be a real and emotional figure who is capable of sharing his feelings of responsibility for the ending of his marriage. It is a loss that both father and son experience, but one that also turns into frozen grief unless it can be talked about. As the scene begins, Billy is lying in bed with his father at his bedside. The boy is blaming himself for his mother's absence.

"Daddy, I'm sorry."

"It's all right."

"Daddy, Mommy left because I was bad."

"That's not it. Your mom loves you very much. It doesn't have anything to do with you. . . . I don't know if this is going to make any sense. . . . I'll try to explain it to you. . . . Okay? I think the reason why mommy left was that, for a long time, I've been trying to make her be a certain kind of a person that I thought she used to be. . . . And she just wasn't like that. And I know, now that I think about it . . . I think that she tried to make me happy. And when she couldn't, she tried to talk to me about it . . . but I wasn't listening 'cause I was too busy. I was too busy just thinking about myself. And I thought all the time that if I was happy, that meant she was happy, and I think underneath that, she was very sad. . . . And she stayed longer than she wanted to, I think, because she loves you so much. And the reason why she couldn't stay any more is because she couldn't stand me, Billy. She didn't leave because of you, she left because of me. . . . Go to sleep now, okay? Good night. Don't let the bed bugs bite."

"Daddy, I love you."

"I love you, too."

Protecting Our Children by Facing Our Pain

Billy is unable to make sense out of the loss of his mother on his own. Left to his own imagination, he predictably blames himself for her leaving. Children under the age of seven are usually magical and egocentric in their thinking. If an important family event occurs, they may attribute it to something that they have said or done.

It is necessary for Ted Kramer to share his own pain and self-blame with his son so that Billy is not burdened with a sense of guilt.

If a father is unable to face his own wounds and his own sense of shame, then he will pass these feelings along to his son who will then be forced to carry them.

Kramer has given Billy a gift by taking adult responsibility for the ending of his marriage. He has taught his son that men are allowed to be vulnerable and talk about these feelings. Ted Kramer has also given his son permission to make mistakes since even he, as an adult, is capable of messing up his marriage and of being imperfect. By not blaming Billy's mother, he has taken his son out of a loyalty conflict in which Billy might feel that he has to decide which of his parents is right and which is wrong. A more aloof father, unable to deal with his wounds, might have only revealed his anger, leaving his son to take on his anger and remorse.

Kramer went through all of the normal phases of mourning that follow an important loss. If we examine the progression of Kramer's feelings after his separation, it can serve as a guide to the process of healing.

1. Ted Kramer first experienced a period of shock and disbelief after his wife left him. Part of him wanted to deny what was happening to him.

2. He next tried to bargain with his wife to return. This was still part of his denial that the separation was really happening to him.

3. Ted Kramer then became angry which showed itself in his initial resentment at having to take full responsibility for his son.

4. Ted then experienced depression when he told his son Billy that he took responsibility for what went wrong.

5. Ted eventually accepted the loss of his marriage and some of his career goals as he took on his role of father and developed a deeper relationship with his son.

This fictional account of a father's failed marriage and his attempt to parent his own son by himself can teach us a great deal about loss and renewal. Ted Kramer was able to experience a broad range of feelings that carried him past his initial anger and into his grief. It is often difficult for men to get past their anger. Since it is one of the few emotions that we are "permitted" to express, it can cover our underlying sadness and remorse. The experience of mourning his losses and also fathering his son became a second chance for Ted Kramer. The humanizing influence of playing a fatherly role allowed him to evolve from a corporate man with no relationship with his son to a nurturing and involved parent.

Early Abandonment: When a Father Chooses to Leave

What happens when a father *chooses* to leave his family and never return? This poses a different problem for the child who has been abandoned.

Brad is a nine-year-old boy who first saw me when he was five. Brad's father had psychiatric problems. He was being treated for a manic depressive disorder involving wide mood swings that were stabilized with the use of the drug Lithium. When Brad was just four-and-a-half years old, his parents' marriage began to fall apart and his father decided to move back to Belgium, his country of origin. After one or two letters and a few phone calls, Brad's father cut off all communication with his son. This severed communication left Brad with the formidable task of trying to make sense of the fact that his father had vanished from his life.

Much of Brad's counseling with me has involved careful planning with his mother about how to help him come to terms with what had befallen him. What type of explanation would make sense to Brad and cause him to feel that he had not brought this on himself? How could we provide Brad with the ideas that would help him to understand the situation and not leave him feeling guilty and powerless?

I spoke with Brad about his father's illness—and explained that it was a disease that sometimes made it very difficult for people to stay connected to the important people in their lives. This made some sense to Brad, but his limited understanding of being ill also made him anxious for the illness to be over so that his father could return.

Brad went through months when he refused to talk about his loss, and I learned to respect a healing process that involved time and patience. There were other times when the loss of a toy or frustration with a game would set off such a torrent of tears that the connection to his underlying father loss became apparent.

Brad is an only child and lives with his mother. Brad's understanding of his loss makes his mother want to ease his pain by giving him the latitude to express himself. On the other hand, she runs the risk of indulging his angry behavior in which he acts out his frustration against her. Underneath Brad's anger is a depression that, at times, has included suicidal ideas.

Brad is the most reflective child with whom I've ever worked, but just below the surface is a reservoir of sadness that is "connected" to his original loss. When he turned eight, he began to talk about how sad he was that he never got to meet either of his two grandfathers—a step removed from missing his father, but still an important emotional connection for him to make.

Brad still becomes very angry when things don't go his way, and I've been working with him on the idea of "disappointment," which is so much a part of his early loss. During the years ahead I feel Brad will be able to understand more about his father and what made him disappear in the way that he did. Brad can also learn to appreciate and value the family that has remained with him and reappraise what his mother has been able to give him in his father's absence.

My own role as Brad's counselor presents a dilemma since I have become a father figure to him without being available in those special ways that fathers, male friends, and relatives can. When I have ended sessions with him temporarily, he always wants to "sign up for next year," and I continue to wonder if he will benefit from separating from me, or simply experience yet another loss of an important male figure in his life.

Childhood abandonment can take many forms and appear in many guises. As adults, we can continue to experience the symptoms of the child who has been abandoned if our fathers have absented themselves through work, substance abuse, or emotional withdrawal. Depression, disappointment, and longing may continue to have an impact on the way we live our lives.

Here are some things that we might learn from Brad and his reactions to abandonment by his father:

- Brad tried to make sense out of his loss, but when he couldn't figure things out, he pushed it out of his mind. As adults, we also *avoid* thinking about what is emotionally painful and difficult to make sense of. The negative side of avoiding the reality of our losses is that while we can have some control over what we are aware of, what we push out of awareness tends to control us.

- Brad would become very angry when he experienced even minor losses, but he wasn't able to make the connection between these reactions and the monumental loss he went through when his father left him. Many of us also live our lives with an angry overlay that keeps our earlier losses unmourned.

- Brad communicates an underlying sadness and a sense of disappointment in his mannerisms and expressions. Many of us also live lives tinged with sadness. Both the sense of overriding disappointment and a "quick fuse" can be the veneer that covers an earlier loss.

- Angry demands and acting out behaviors don't help Brad. In children or adults, activity can distract us temporarily, but will not make the grief disappear.

Brad's emotional responses to his father's abandonment are not that different from the lifelong reactions to loss that many adults suffer. We are all capable of denying the impact of loss, using anger to avoid having to grieve, and living a life colored with a sadness that we never understand.

Adult Sons and Their Fathers: Deepening the Bonds

Shockingly, of the many men whom I have interviewed and counseled over the past eighteen years, none have claimed to have had a close relationship with their fathers. However, all of the men who grew up with a father in the home, or had regular visitations with a father, believed that they had a good sense of who their father was. Fathers were usually seen as predictable, even though they were almost never viewed as available in the right way. Perhaps it is this fixed and negative perception of their fathers that has made these men find it so difficult to establish closer relationships with them as adults. The more I spoke with men and counseled them, the more I realized that their ideas about their fathers were frozen at a time in their pasts when they were seven, nine, or sixteen years of age. Like old encyclopedias that one might find in the attic, these men were filled with ideas and information about their fathers that no longer applied.

Some of the men whom I have seen for counseling were unable or unwilling to approach their fathers in a new way. Others have gone on to do significant family of origin work in the process of updating their relationships with their fathers. Their new ideas about their fathers nearly always brought about some new sense about themselves. These are the second chances that become available to us as adults that so many allow to slip away.

Albert, a family therapist, was one man who was able to create a new relationship with his father as an adult. Albert's parents separated when he was two, and he grew up in the custody of his mother. Albert saw his father regularly on weekends, but he was never raised in his father's household. Albert got to know who his father was, but it was understood by all the people in his life that his relationship with his father was a secondary bond. The message from his mother and her side of the family came across clearly to Albert:

"It's okay to love your father, but, remember, he and his family are different from us. They're not concerned about you the way that we are."

Albert's father and his family also had their set views about the role his mother played in the divorce. The divorce had created two camps in which Albert's loyalties were being tested and divided.

In his book on masculinity, *Iron John*, poet Robert Bly writes about the difficulties of a man trying to get to know about his father by speaking to his mother:

> You're not going to get a straight picture of your father out of your mother, nor will you get a straight picture of your mother from your father.

Bly goes on to say:

> If a male is brought up mainly with his mother, he will see his father through his mother's eyes and develop a "wounded" image of his father based on the mother's observations of his behaviors.

The universal theme that Bly leads up to is that, in order to grow up, we need to find out who our parents are through our own eyes, unmediated by anyone else's perceptions. Nobody else can do this for us. It is a purely self-motivated activity.

At age nineteen, Albert was away at college, feeling depressed and lost. He knew that he needed to reconnect with his father, but he wanted this adult part of their relationship to be apart from anything his mother might feel or say. He wanted to have a separate relationship with both of his parents, but every time he considered getting closer to his father, he felt that he was being disloyal to his mother. It still felt that he "belonged" to his mother and would be hurting her if he established a deeper connection with his dad.

Albert decided to write a letter to his father. It wasn't a long letter, but it was a very important one that made it clear: "There is a lot more that I want to say." The letter was the beginning of a new phase in both Albert's life and in the life of his father. It was a statement that Albert wanted to get to know who his father was through his own eyes as an adult. Also, it was Albert's father's second chance to be a better father to his son and to be accepted by Albert beyond the ashes of the failed marriage in which he had grown up.

Fathers need to reconnect with their adult sons as much as the sons need to maintain ongoing, independent relationships with their fathers.

13

LEARNING FROM
OUR CHILDREN

*If a man, even a fatherless father, will let himself learn
from child rearing rather than just trying to control or perfect
his children, they can carry him through all the stages of
human development.*

Frank Pitman, *Man Enough*

WHAT IS IT LIKE for a father to spend time with his children?
Certainly it is not the same experience for all men. But
Alex, a partner in a small electronics parts company who had two
young sons, described it to me this way:

> When I'm at home with my kids, I feel that I should be some-
> where else. My mind jumps back and forth between what's
> going on with my business to my children. I know that I'm
> supposed to be spending quality time with them, but I just
> can't seem to stay focused on what's going on in front of me.

Alex spends most of his long work days on the telephone
moving inventories and making business arrangements. He lives
with the feeling that his work is never done. Therefore, his mind
races on no matter where his body happens to be at the moment.

Alex understands that he is expected to be attentive to his sons, but he has trouble putting his knowledge into practice. Rather than a pleasure to be savored, he feels that the time he spends with his children is like the next shift in a very long work week.

Is Alex one of a large number of men who have been labeled workaholics? Or is he "an anxious overachiever" who can never allow himself to slow down for fear of failing? Maybe he's just a member of the group of fathers who have not yet learned how to relax and enjoy being a father. However we view his problem, my work with men has led me to believe that there is a piece of Alex in each of us. In encouraging the fathers whom I coach to develop a self-focus, I have gained a clearer picture of men's stream of consciousness as they go about their daily activities. The following is a description of one father's thoughts as he played ball with his eleven-year-old son.

> I'll speak to Jack in the morning. If we don't get moving on the body work, we'll have nothing to sell come September. The lawn looks like hell. I should probably get to it along with the garage door which is rotting off its hinges. Now, getting back to the shop, I'll order more paint, but the money for that might have to come out of household dollars until the cash flow improves later in the month. . . .

On some level in this monologue the son knows that his father has absented himself from their activity together. He may not know the inner workings of his father's mind, but he understands that his dad is not with him in spirit. He may see his father's worried expression as a sign that he's not doing something right, or he may have just come to see his father's preoccupation as a big sign that says "Do Not Disturb."

Sometimes family structure or tradition creates a situation in which one partner, often the father, is the primary wage earner. I have found that it is crucial for both partners to participate in financial decision-making, regardless of who earns the most money. It is critical that each partner understands the household budget and plans how discretionary money will be used.

If one partner is in charge of the family finances, then he or she is in danger of becoming an isolated warrior who is absent in other areas of family life.

One-Dimensional Dads

The father who finds his mind wandering from his children back to his job may see himself in the traditional father role of family financial manager. He may reflect the generations of fathers that came before him in his feeling that "breadwinning" is where his focus ought to be.

The underlying belief that many fathers still hold is that children are not their equal responsibility. Where children are concerned, some fathers feel that men are temporary workers who fill in until they are relieved by their wives. At that point, they can return to their primary role as breadwinner or maintenance man. This attitude is held by both men and women.

I have found that the father who sees himself as the monetary provider and second parent generally has a narrow concept of what it means to be a father and a man. His "code of behavior" may include the following beliefs:

A good father is a good provider whose place is at work. He may help out at home, but he is not in charge of leisure, social planning, or what is going on between family members.
A good father is in charge of competitive activities.

He knows the rules, encourages winning, and is the one in the family who keeps score.

Good fathers are tough, consistently self-reliant, and always in control. They do not let on when they are frightened or reveal when they feel weak.

Men who conform to the profile of the one-dimensional father are those who tend to create rigid family systems in which very little interchange goes on between family members. In such a family people are just too afraid of being judged to share their feelings or ideas. These fathers end up as emotional outsiders while all interactions flow between the mother and children. Sons in this type of family almost always adopt their father's "code of silence," and the fathers are thwarted in their adult development because they are too guarded to learn anything new about themselves while in the presence of their children.

Doing a Project with Children

Fathers who want to move away from a preoccupation with work or a rigid way of relating to their children will not benefit from being told by others that they "just need to relax." If these fathers could relax, they would do so with their children around or without.

I have found that it is beneficial for a father to be able to do a planned project with his children while he maintains a degree of self-focus. In doing this, a father can improve his relationship with his children while he learns something new about himself. If he can recall what it was like to do things with his own father, he will usually gain a better understanding of why he handles situations the way he does with his own children.

When I was a child, I realized very early that doing something *with* Dad had a lot to do with him and very little to do with me. I can remember how I wanted to build a knock-hockey board when I was eleven, and approaching my father with a request for help. The project was completed within a week, but I had little to do with the work itself. I looked on while my father measured the Masonite board and sawed the side panels. Part of me wanted to say, "This is my idea—show me how I can do some of this!" But the part of me that learned that he needed to act in this way to fulfill his own needs stood quietly on the sidelines and remained silent. What might have been a father-son activity which involved instruction and participation turned into another isolating experience for us both. In the past, when I have done school assignments with my children, I became aware of how similar I am to my father. For instance, I had almost completed one such project which my younger daughter brought home with her when she said to me, "What can I do before you finish the whole thing by yourself?"

Fathers generally get stuck in two areas when they engage in projects with their children. These areas have to do with becoming overly focused on the completion of the task in front of them, and not maintaining enough self-awareness. We may need to ask ourselves the following questions again and again:

1. Am I balancing the work of the project—the planning and execution of the task itself—with a dialogue between myself and my child? Is he or she involved in this project and are we relating to each other?

2. What am I going through on a "gut level" while I'm doing this project? Am I feeling rushed? Tense? Having to get it perfect? The feelings that we get while we are doing something with our kids may be the signposts of what we are carrying with us from our relationships with our fathers.

Dealing with Our Own Impatience

Robert is a lawyer with a prestigious New York law firm. He comes from a working class background and has moved up in his career through his own persistent effort. Robert expects a great deal from himself and has set high standards for his three children. His expectations are certainly part of what has motivated them to excel academically, but his impatience with everyone in his family is what brought him into counseling with me.

Whenever Robert participated in activities with his children, there was a tense, pressured atmosphere that permeated his home. In one counseling session, Robert described working on a makeshift tree house with his ten-year-old son Michael, that ended in a disturbing family scene. Michael was discovered crying in his bedroom by his mother, who decided that it was time for her husband to get some help. When Robert related what went on between him and his son, I was able to understand how things got so out of hand. Robert approaches life with his own logic and becomes impatient when things don't go his way. He knew very little about how to build a tree house, but he found himself becoming irritated as time passed and the job wasn't getting done. I sensed that Michael was upset because he had begun to feel that he had done something to bring on his father's anger, but could not figure out what that "something" was.

I asked Robert if he understood why he felt it was so important for him to get things done quickly when he was with his family. I also asked where all this pressure about time was coming from. I wondered whether Robert would be able to put aside his own desperate need to succeed long enough to grasp the emotional impact of his behavior on his children.

I knew that I needed to remain focused on very practical solutions if I was going to coach Robert toward a new position with his children. He was so invested in getting things accomplished quickly and efficiently that any suggestion I might make about a change "process" would certainly not be welcomed. Nevertheless, there were background facts I needed to learn. I asked Robert, Who else in his first family might also have had that quality? It did not take Robert long to understand his own impatience was related to that of his silent but demanding father. As the eldest son of five brothers and sisters, Robert had always been a very high achiever, giving his family an aura of success. His father had approved of his son's hard work and achievements with a nod and a gesture, but had never openly acknowledged the effort that it had taken for Robert to work his way through law school and become a partner in his firm. The last thing Robert wanted to consider was spending time alone with his father. However, that was exactly what I felt he needed to do. I pressed him to have a one-time meeting with his father. I told him his report on the meeting would help me do my family assessment as his counselor, but Robert continued to resist and told me: "My father is just not a talker. He gets his messages across to other people through my mother. I don't think I've ever had a real conversation with him."

I continued to press by asking, "How does he spend his time since he retired?"

"According to my mother, he just tinkers with his car. He's been doing that every Saturday morning for as long as I can remember."

"Have you ever tinkered on the car together with your father?"

"I used to help out until I was fifteen," Robert explained, "when I finally decided that I had enough of his scenes when things didn't go his way."

I knew that Robert would gain more from a direct experience with his father than any insight I could hope to provide. I asked Robert if he would just drop over to his father's house the following Saturday morning while his father was working on the car. Finally Robert relented and said he would be willing to do this one time, but he knew that there was nothing to be gained from the experience. I promised not to suggest that he do it a second time if he would agree to approach the visit in the way that I would prescribe.

I asked Robert if he thought he was capable of just standing by the car as his father was working on it in the same way he did when he was a child. All Robert was required to do was observe everything that his father said or did during their visit along with his own reactions.

When Robert came to see me for our next session, he had much to say about what had gone on when he visited his father. "My father hasn't changed very much over the years. He was still working on his car the way he always did." But Robert had changed. He was no longer a frightened little boy worried about getting Daddy angry. He could step back and learn from what was going on in front of him, if he could just control his own reactions to his father.

Robert reported that when he first arrived that morning, his father hardly acknowledged his presence. The older man just continued to putter, keeping his head under the hood of the car. Periodically, Robert's father would grumble about something that wasn't going the way he wanted it to, and Robert noticed that he had a habit of continually looking at his watch. The only time he spoke to his son was to ask him to give him a tool that was not immediately within his reach. One time when Robert didn't hand him the tool quickly enough his father became impatient and said, "Didn't you hear me? I said the small pliers."

Robert didn't say anything at that point. He just continued to observe his father and his own reactions as I had instructed. He recalled how upset he would get as a ten-year-old working with his father. It was so important at the time to get things right so that his dad would give him a nod of approval. But, thirty-two years later, Robert was able to observe this very tense man grow impatient and angry while realizing for the first time that it had nothing to do with him. Later, while standing with his father over the engine, Robert ventured a suggestion.

"You might do better with a larger wrench," he said to his dad.

His father grunted, "That might work" and then went back to what he was doing.

To a casual observer, not much happened on that Saturday morning. An elderly father did some work on his car, his middle-aged son observed him, and a few words were exchanged. But for Robert something very important occurred. He had watched his father grow angry without feeling any sense of blame—something that he was never able to do as a child. And he had offered an opinion to his father, another new experience for the younger man. Even more important for Robert and his family, he was able to see his own impatience with his children in a new light.

Several weeks later, Robert said to me, "I'm not really any different from my father. What he did to me around the car, I've done a hundred times to Michael and the others."

I was impressed with Robert's courage and willingness to look at his own behavior in the face of the pain that he had experienced in his father's home. My coaching of Robert involved keeping the connection alive between what he had observed going on between his father and himself, and what he was capable of repeating with his own children. For a time, whenever Robert was planning to spend time with any of his children, I would remind him of how to approach it.

"I'd like you to spend five minutes just thinking about your father," I said. "I'd like you to think about his mannerisms, what he would say or do and anything else about him that you can recall."

Robert's impatience and anger in the presence of his children subsided gradually over the next seven months. He visited his father four times during that period and he was able to have several real conversations with him. However, near the end of the seventh month Robert started to complain to me about feeling depressed.

Handling Our Grief

We usually think of depression as something bad. It can involve low energy, poor concentration, and a sense of hopelessness. In Robert's case, though, I didn't view his depression as anything more than a reflection of the changes going on in his life, things that he was facing for the first time. I saw it as a part of a sadness and grief that he had to experience in order to move forward. Grief is present whenever there is a loss, but it often gets covered over with other emotions if we are unable to mourn that thing or person that we may be missing. One could ask, "What did Robert have to grieve about?" He was a very successful lawyer with a large home and a family. However, he was also a tense, impatient man who had spent his life angrily pushing away the important people in his life, and he was now viewing the heavy price he had paid for his behavior.

Men have been taught to hide their grief behind their anger. They will often suffer secondary losses by keeping loved ones at a distance with their rage.

Robert had never had a father with whom he could communicate—a parent who could have offered him guidance and approval but instead communicated impatience and rage. Robert had managed to survive this loss by pushing his feelings back and moving forward with his career and his life. But, on another level, Robert had carried his father's way of relating to people into his own relations with his new family. Robert was repeating with his children exactly what was done to him. Remaining cut off from his father only served to intensify the pattern that he was playing out. Visiting his father again as an adult brought Robert face to face with another isolated man, like himself, who had spent his life keeping family members at a distance. In making the connection between himself and his father, Robert could no longer spend time with his children without feeling his own father's loss.

Giving What We Didn't Get

If we are at last able to face our losses and allow grief to be a part of our lives, then fathering our children will become a meaningful process, and we will grow from the experience. For most of us, being a real father obligates us to give to our children the love and relatedness we did not receive. If we continue to give despite our deprivations from the past, we will be able to cleanse and heal our old wounds and prevent them from festering. Learning from our children means being aware of the memories and emotions evoked within ourselves.

FATHERS
AND
SEXUALITY

IT MAY SEEM THAT sex is an adult topic that should have no place in a fatherhood discussion. Yet, in my work, I have discovered that the sexual relations between adults in a family affect what happens in the rest of the family as well.

What goes on between mothers and fathers in the area of intimacy and sexuality has a significant impact on the emotional well-being of their children.

I have consulted with parents who stopped having a sexual relationship with each other and whose marriages no longer involved physical affection or emotional intimacy. Some are having extra-marital affairs and say that they are staying in the marriage "only for the sake of the children." They are anxious to see me about problems their children may be having in school, but they are unwilling to take a deeper look at the problems in their marriage or to consider the effect these problems have on the entire family. The dilemma that I face in working with this type of family is that, if I agree to only focus on the children's behavior as "the problem," then I am going along with the parents' denial of the impact of their loveless marriage on their family. It is my experience that, over the years of their development, the children will inevitably fill the vacuum of the sexual and emotional needs that are not being met in their parents' marriage.

The most common family triangle involves two parents and one or more of their children. The more chronic the distance and hostility in the marriage, the more the children must adapt their behaviors to reduce the tensions between their parents.

As a counselor, I have seen many children recruited into "the family problem." When the child acts up in school or at home, it looks like the problem is in the child's behavior. According to the parent and/or school administrators, if I can just get the child to stop "acting up," things will improve for everyone. That is almost never the solution. The acting out child is a *symptom* of what else is wrong in the family and is only a diversion for the parents who are usually unwilling to examine the conflicts in their marriage.

My Family's Sexual Triangle

In my family, there was a "no talk" rule about sex. Nobody ever stated that sex was a forbidden topic, but I learned over the years that asking certain questions seemed to upset my parents or make them uneasy. I had no way of knowing at age seven or eight that my mother and father were having problems that had nothing to do with me. I grew up in an emotional environment with a great deal of sexual jealousy and rage, and I positioned myself between my father and mother to act as a buffer for their marital pain.

A child who is triangled into his parents' relationship is a victim of emotional incest whether he is physically violated or not. He is a prisoner of a family bind that saps his creative energy and prevents him from feeling good about himself. In my child's mind I reasoned if I were to move closer to my father I would be disloyal to my mother, and if I took my mother's side, I would be in an alliance against my father. As I grew to adolescence, my budding ideas about sexuality and relationships had already become entangled in the web of my parents' mistrust and fear.

I have since come to understand that the behavior problems I began to exhibit in school were, in large part, a reflection of my parents' inability to negotiate their adult needs and development within the emotional boundaries of their marriage.

My home was not a healthy and vibrant place for me to grow up because my parents were not growing into their marriage.

The relative health of the marriage between a father and mother sets the emotional tone for the rest of the family. In separated families, it is the capacity of each parent to reconstitute his or her life and form new relationships that enables the children to renew their trust in people and the world. If the intimacy needs of the adults in a family are met and they are growing into their relationships, the entire family will benefit. If, on the other hand, the two parties are in a state of cold war and the relationship lacks intimacy or is unsatisfying, the couple's sexual feelings will go underground and surface elsewhere in the system. In fact, the relationship between fatherhood and sexuality is really about developing our adult capacity for intimacy so that our children's lives are not contaminated by our unmet needs.

One of the truly important gifts that a father can give to his children is his effort to maintain an intimate relationship with his partner.

For too long, we as a society have attempted to compartmentalize what goes on in one part of a person's life from what goes on in the rest of it. We have pretended that we can create a satisfactory environment for our children in families in which the primary adult relationship is not working to create an intimate, growth producing experience for its partners.

Men and Intimacy

The word "intimacy" is bandied about in our popular culture of talk shows and magazines. But what does it mean to engage in "intimate behavior," and are we all speaking about the same thing when we say that "intimacy" is something that we want?

I grew up in a generation in which the conventional wisdom told us that:

"Women give sex to get love." (This probably means that women primarily need an emotional connection in a relationship.)

"Men give love to get sex." (This probably means that men are willing to show that they are emotionally connected to achieve their "sexual goal.")

This *give* to get approach to relationships between men and women sets us up to believe that there are innate differences in our needs for emotional closeness and sexual union.

A poll of women in the 1950s would probably have found that "emotional openness" was construed to be the main ingredient of an intimate relationship. A similar poll of men of that era would likely have equated intimacy with something more physical—sex itself, or whatever is a prelude to sex. I believe these attitudes are changing. In my more recent counseling experiences with both young men and women, I have found that the needs for separateness and togetherness are fairly equal. And that the differences between the sexes regarding the need for emotional closeness and sexuality in relationships break down as they grow older.

The word "intimacy" as I am using it has much more to do with the *quality* of what occurs *within* the individuals in a relationship than the specific behaviors people engage in. For men in particular, the development of "intimacy skills" has profound implications for the quality of their marriages and the fulfillment of sexual desires that occurs between themselves and their wives. It also impacts on the lives of their children in direct and indirect ways.

One important intimacy skill has to do with the willingness to tell the important people in our lives what we are feeling, including our likes and our dislikes, our desires and our fears. Relationships only move forward if a person continues to disclose information based upon his decision to do so, and not on whether his partner approves or disapproves of what he is going to say.

David Schnarch, a pioneer in the field of sex and marital therapy, in his book *Constructing the Sexual Crucible*, has identified two levels of intimacy that have a major impact on the quality of relationships and family life:

LEVEL ONE INTIMACY:
At this level, people depend upon each other to validate what they say or do. An intimate conversation might sound something like this: "I'll have to tell you something about me, but you also have to tell me something about you. I'll open up if you do, but don't expect me to if you won't."

LEVEL TWO INTIMACY:
At this level, intimacy is more inner driven and less depen-dent on what a partner might say or think. It might sound something like this: "I've decided that I wanted to tell you something about myself that I've never shared before. . . . I just wanted you to know this about me."

Or, it might be expressed as: "I'd like to try something with you that we've never done before."

Level Two intimacy is an expression of self that does not depend on the validation of the other partner.

Married couples often complain about sexual boredom and think back to the "good old days when everything was new and exciting." They may say that their sex life has lost its novelty. However, how do people bring about novelty in a long term rela-tionship? Somebody has to be willing to innovate. There will never be innovation at Level One intimacy in which partners depend upon each other for validation. Innovation will only occur if a man or woman is willing to disclose what he or she wants without needing the approval of his partner. Higher levels of self-disclosure where *we validate our own wishes and needs* fuel the forward motion of a sexual relationship and create the potential for new and intense erotic experiences. At higher levels of dif-ferentiation in an intimate sexual relationship, the experience is neither consensual nor smooth. The process of defining a self in an intimate relationship is based upon our capacity to tolerate conflict and anxiety in the interest of growth.

A Father's Development and His Children's Sexuality

There is an important connection between a father's capacity to move toward a higher level of intimate self-disclosure with his partner and his ability to define who he is to his children.

A father who evolves sexually and grows in intimacy within his marriage will be better able to bring this part of himself into his relationship with his children. A father who avoids the sexual issues in his marriage will usually retreat from the topics of sex and intimacy with his children, and the message that sex is shameful or taboo will be communicated by its blatant omission over time. In order for our children to be able to have a dialogue with us about who they are in this part of their lives, we, as fathers, need to come out of hiding and extend ourselves and our knowledge to them. What often makes it difficult for us men to be open with our children is our confusion about sex. Our views come from the messages that we received from our original families and society during our childhood.

Men's Sexual Confusion

In my interviews with men, I have found that the area least talked about between fathers and sons is the area of sexuality. In follow-up discussions with interviewees, I came to understand that one of the reasons for men's lack of communication might be their own confusion about their sexual feelings. It became clear to me that, if men had a better understanding of their own sexuality, this would not be the problem it seems to be.

One source of male confusion is a lack of knowledge about sex. Robert Pasick, a researcher and author on men's issues, discusses in his book, *Awakening from the Deep Sleep*, men's general lack of information in this area:

> We are both fascinated and confused by sex. A recent Roper/Kinsey Institute poll confirmed that men lack basic information about sex. Among males taking the test, 55 percent answered less than half of the eighteen multiple choice questions correctly. Only 10 percent of the respondents correctly answered 80 percent or more of the items on fundamental sexual information.

A second source of male confusion has to do with messages from our childhood that tell us that sex is shameful and should be kept a secret from others. This conflicts with the current trend that encourages men to be more open and candid about their lives. The family "no talk" rule that was standard for so many of us during childhood can remain a powerful injunction against expressing our adult feelings and needs.

As the "instrumental ones" in our society, men have been trained to question whether they are "measuring up" or "performing up to par." In viewing sex in terms of performance, men often find it difficult to experience pleasure or achieve intimacy. The anxiety associated with "performance" is so agonistic to sex and intimacy that it is one of the primary causes of sexual dysfunction. In looking at sex as an act to be performed rather than as part of a relationship process, men frequently run into conflicts with their partners.

Women often complain of feeling used and "turned off" sexually when they feel that their partners are too focused on the act, rather than the emotional connection. It is ironic that a man's feeling that he was unable to "satisfy" his partner is often fueled by his anxious focus on his "performance" instead of a realistic concern about what is going on in the relationship as a whole.

Understanding the Messages We Received

Positive change is always based on greater self-understanding. The need for more general information about sex can be met by gathering a good reading list. However, only specific knowledge about our own background can help us to understand the sexual beliefs and behaviors that we bring to our relationships. Consider this question:

What were the messages regarding sex that you received from society as a child, adolescent, and young adult?

The "messages" that we received from society have to do with the era in which we were raised. A man who grew to adulthood during the 1960s and 1970s, as I did, was imprinted with the values of what has been referred to as the "sexual revolution." Although the "revolution" didn't last very long, it promoted the idea that it was good to experiment with different life styles. The more repressive sexual messages from my family were at least temporarily supplanted by the values of sexual pleasure and freedom. Whatever era we grew up in, we tend to incorporate some of its values and carry them with us into our later relationships.

People who were adolescents or young adults in the 1980s have received a different message about sex and relationships than I did a decade earlier. With the advent of AIDS and a generally more conservative political climate, they have heard a great deal about "family values," "chastity," and "safe sex." The notion that sex is not to be explored beyond the safety of a monogamous relationship is once again a prevalent ideal of our culture.

Thinking about the times in which we grew up and the "cultural messages" that we were exposed to can become an integral part of self-understanding. It can tell us how we developed our attitudes about the way a man is expected to behave in a sexual relationship. For instance, the myths and images of how men and women are "supposed" to act when intimate with each other have been transmitted to us in movies, popular music, television shows, and the way products are advertised and sold. Some other valuable questions to ask ourselves about the formation of our attitudes surrounding sex and intimacy are:

What messages did my ethnic group give me about sex?

What did my religion instill in me about sex and intimacy?

What values or attitudes did the schools that I attended teach me about sex?

What did I learn about sex from my peer groups as I was growing up?

Messages from Home

The most powerful and enduring attitudes and beliefs that we have about sex have come to us through our parents. What we experienced growing up in close proximity to our parents' marriage or other adult relationships forms the basis for our deepest feelings about what it means to be intimate with a partner. Even when we try our hardest to create a different type of relationship from the one our parents had, the indelible marks of their marriage color our daily life. It is our position as a child viewing our parents' marriage that determines how we come to understand and appreciate the normal boundaries that exist between people. It is here that we learn how to act in a relationship with another person while also maintaining a separate life. During times of high anxiety and emotional intensity, there is *always* the danger of pulling a child into the middle of a marital conflict. To the degree that parents are able to contain their conflicts within their marriage and limit the *triangling* of their children, their children will feel safe and protected in relationship to others. This is also a crucial determinant in how safe and pleasurable future intimate relationships will feel to those children.

The ideas that we get from our families about the nature of relationships are so pervasive that we may feel that is the way things are "supposed to be." Our rules and behaviors about relating to others usually receive their first major challenge when we decide to get married. After the initial romantic phase in which we are oblivious to dissimilarity, we are forced to contend with a partner who operates by a different set of rules about how to manage closeness, conflict, and intimacy. It is during this normal phase of marital disillusion and discord that differences need to be negotiated. It is also at this point in marriage that many couples either break up or seek outside help. The couples who come to me for help in this area almost always point the finger of blame at their partners. They invariably experience a sense of betrayal about the gap between whom they thought they had married and that person sitting next to them on the couch in my office. What they could not possibly understand at that moment is that their marriage is quite healthy and is doing exactly what it is supposed to do—it is providing them with the opportunity to grow up and establish an intimate relationship.

Whether or not a couple is able to begin to appreciate each other's differences and to negotiate new positions has to do with each partner's level of differentiation.

If even one of the partners is able to manage his or her *reactivity* well enough to gain some *self-focus*, the marriage will be able to move forward over time. My task as a marital counselor and coach is to help him or her calm down reactivity and focus *away* from the partner and more on the self. If I am able to help each of them develop a better understanding of the rules, roles, attitudes, and beliefs that each of them brings to their marriage, then I know that I have done my job and that their marriage has a good chance to survive. The following questions have been helpful for couples who are trying to define their attitudes and roles in a marriage, but need more information about themselves in the area of intimacy and sexuality.

1. How did people in your family of origin express affection toward each other? How often and under what circumstances did it occur?

2. Did people in your family use physical touch as a means of expression? What did you see going on between the adults in your family and between the adults and children?

3. Did people in your family know how other members felt about things? How did people express themselves when it came to feelings?

4. What were your family's attitudes about the body? Were the

body and bodily functions supposed to be hidden or exposed? Could they be talked about?

5. Was sex a topic that could be brought up and discussed? If something was communicated about sex, under what circumstances was it done?

6. What were your thoughts and feelings about your parents' sexual activities? What did you see or hear that gave you those impressions?

7. Were there members of your extended family—your aunts, uncles, and grandparents—who gave you other messages about sex and intimacy? Are there family "stories" or "secrets" about the sexual activity of family members?

8. What went on between you and any brothers or sisters in the area of affection, sexuality, and intimacy? What were your parents' attitudes and involvement in what was discussed?

9. How were the "rules" and expectations about sex and expressiveness different depending upon whether you were a boy or a girl growing up in your family? If there were a number of children, did your order of birth affect the type of message you received?

Our families inculcate us with ways of relating to others that encompass our sexuality and much of what we say and do in our relationships. The family "style" may be emotionally distant and cold, sensuous and warm, or rigid and controlling. We may come from families that are isolated and let very little outside information in, or families with very "loose boundaries" in which outsiders seem to come and go as they please. Whatever the style, these are the family systems in which we were formed and where we learned the rules of attachment and intimacy that we carry with us into adulthood and our fatherhood.

Becoming Intimate with Our Children

As we begin to consider what we bring with us from our families of origin to our families of procreation, we become aware of how much is determined by what came before. However, it is the central thesis of this book that the more knowledgeable an individual becomes about his multi-generational past, the less doomed he is to repeat it in predictable, programmed ways.

A father who is aware of what he carries with him from his first family will be able to understand the actions that he may repeat with his own children. In the case history that follows, a father whom I originally saw for a marital problem was encouraged to examine what he was communicating to his children regarding intimacy and sex.

Andrew first contacted me by phone and set up an appointment to discuss his concerns about sex and marriage. He told me that he was forty-two years old and an associate professor of economics at a large college. He wanted reassurance that everything he told me would be kept "confidential" and asked if I thought it would be all right if he saw me without his wife's knowledge. I told him that it would be okay for him to see me initially without telling his wife, but the issue of secrecy in his marriage would probably be important to examine. Andrew agreed to my terms and we set up our first session two weeks later.

Andrew's relationship with his new partner followed a failed marriage that left him with a joint custody agreement and large child support payments. He resented that, although his ex-wife had been the unfaithful one in their marriage, he was the one told by the judge to pay the family's financial burdens. He described his current marriage as a more mature relationship than his first one, but he worried about his diminishing desire for sex following a passionate courtship.

The teenage children from his first marriage were Jason, aged twelve, who was described to me as "shy and reserved," and

Allie, aged sixteen, who was more outgoing. Allie was involved with a boy from the local high school. The joint custody agreement had the children shuttling back and forth between households twice a month, but the divorced parents seemed like they were reasonably aware of the need to keep the children out of the inevitable conflicts that are a part of every separation and divorce.

The problem that Andrew presented in his first session had to do with sexual desire between him and his second wife. Although he had his share of sexual issues and attitudes from his past, this was the type of problem that needed to be understood as part of the marital "system" that the new husband and wife were in the process of creating together. The fact that Andrew wanted to deal with it apart from his wife reflected his own discomfort with sex and his feelings of inadequacy in this area. I spent the remaining part of our first session dispelling the idea that sexual issues in the marriage could be kept a secret from his wife, and he was able to consider including her in future sessions.

The meetings that were eventually set up with Andrew and his wife, Elaine, focused more on what was not being talked about between them than an identifiable sexual "dysfunction." It became clear to me as I worked with Andrew that the wish for secrecy he brought to our initial session was also the quality that stood in the way of a genuinely intimate relationship with his second wife. As they began to talk about the loneliness and blank spaces in their marriage, some of the emotional barriers that they had created came down and they were able to view and consider the connection between intimate self-disclosure and passion in a relationship.

We might have ended our sessions at this point with the couple having an invigorated marriage and a better understanding of how they could easily slip back into a pattern of secrecy and mutual avoidance. However, I decided to invite Andrew back for another meeting which had to do with his role as a father. He hadn't requested help in this area, but I knew that it was an important area for him to consider and one which, if he kept "secret," would have ramifications for his marriage as well.

Andrew returned for three more sessions in which we examined his relationship with his son and daughter. I specifically focused on the silence and secrecy that existed between himself and his children in the area of sexuality and emotional relationships. We explored the messages of shame and sin regarding sex that he had received from his family of origin and the parochial education that he had experienced. I wondered with him how he might have passed these messages along to his children—not by what he had said to them about sex, but by what he was *not* saying.

Because of AIDS and other dangers, talking about sexual activity to a teenager has become more of a life and death issue than it has ever been. Therefore, I confronted Andrew with the task of speaking to his daughter about her involvement with her boyfriend and his concern as her father for her safety. He was adamant that it was a mother's responsibility to speak to her daughter about "sensitive topics," but I encouraged him to participate. The coaching of a man in the areas of his most intensely felt shame and anxiety is painstaking work fraught with resistance, and my encouragement always seemed to work best in the form of a question: "What would it be like for you to bring up your concern about your daughter's relationship with her boyfriend?"

And I added, "If you decided to bring it up, how might you phrase the question?"

Eventually, my hypothetical questions were turned into action by Andrew who was able to raise the issue of sexual activity with his daughter. As it has turned out in so many situations where someone is willing to try a new approach, there was an initial discomfort when Andrew first spoke to her, followed by an openness and a relief by the daughter at being able to talk to her father about her life. Sexuality became the secondary issue as

Allie revealed to her father her feelings that he had never been interested or approved of her since she had become a teenager. Andrew was also able to reveal to his daughter the discomfort that he had always felt about sex and intimacy from his own background.

Andrew reached out to his twelve-year-old son in a different way than to his daughter. Respecting Jason's shyness, Andrew told him that he would be available to speak about sexuality and relationships when his son was ready to do so. With my encouragement, Andrew also apologized for not having been as open and communicative as he might have been. He came to the realization that he had never before admitted being wrong about anything to his children, and he was able to connect this desire to always be right to his own father's rigid and authoritarian behavior during his childhood.

Achieving intimacy with one's children or loved ones often has to do with striking a balance between different parts of ourselves. In only expressing his competent side, Andrew was not relating to the part of himself that, at times, felt inadequate and vulnerable. He was not allowing others to get to know this part of him.

Movement toward greater intimacy involves expressing both our weakness and our competence, our vulnerability as well as our strength.

15

FAMILY LOYALTIES

A PATRIARCHAL SOCIETY IS marked by the supremacy of the father in the family or the clan. It is a system of male privilege that has been in existence for millennia and is now in its declining years. In societies and families organized around the principles of male power, allegiance to the "king" is of paramount importance. Disagreement with a father is not viewed as mere disobedience but may be seen as an act of disloyalty or even betrayal.

In the play *Fiddler on the Roof*, the character Tevyeh is a loving and benign father until one of his daughters chooses to marry outside of their Jewish religion. At that point Tevyeh's heart hardens and he exercises his paternal right to banish her from the clan. In Tevyeh's mind she has betrayed her community by being disloyal to his faith.

Ivan Boszormenyi-Nagy in *Invisible Loyalties* examines the issue of loyalty in families in a different light. He views families as having an underlying system of justice that insures obligations and emotional "debts" get settled as "accounts" passed down from one generation to the next. In this way, the scapegoated and exploited child in one generation turns into the possessive, suffocating parent in the next one: "In family life people are too close to an inescapable accounting of justice to bypass the guilt over abuse of power."

Nagy's view of the world, just as Bowen's, stipulates that the "good guys" and "bad guys" in a family are never allowed to retain their fairy tale purity. It is our loyalty to these family distortions that prevents us from growing up and becoming adults in our own right. Emancipation from one' family's "unsettled accounts" is based upon a resolution of the resentments and contempt that we may harbor toward our parents. Achieving it is predicated on knowledge and understanding about how one's family has managed its affairs over time.

Joe is a client of mine who grew up in a harsh, patriarchal family, and his loyalty issues are never far below the surface. I felt that redefining the meaning of loyalty and betrayal in his family would become his key to defining a more solid sense of himself.

Taking New Positions

Joe is a social services supervisor. He was thirty-two years old and lived with his wife and three-year-old son when he first began to see me. The past years have been difficult ones for him. He was referred to me for counseling after spending three weeks away from his family at an alcohol rehabilitation center.

Joe first came to see me right after becoming aware that he had a drinking problem, something he had avoided looking at for his entire adult life. Through our work together he began realizing how stressful his early family environment had been. He began to understand how the emotional impact of his unresolved issues with his father continued to impact his present life.

"Be loyal to father at all costs" was the injunction with which Joe had grown up. He needed to break away from his father's set of rules and expectations in order to become his own person.

There were two events that preceded Joe's work with me that tipped his fragile emotional balance and forced him to face the way he abused alcohol when things became too stressful for him. The first incident involved a disgruntled client at work who was furious about a ruling that Joe had made on the client's application for public assistance. It was only on rare occasions that Joe had to deal with an applicant who refused to accept his determination and also rejected the option to appeal. The man in question made some veiled threats against Joe and then left the office, cursing.

Joe hadn't given the incident much thought until he found the windshield of his car shattered two days later. Under a piece of glass on the hood of his car Joe found a scrap of paper with a death threat scrawled across it. Joe called the police and handed the paper over to the investigators. Joe installed alarms in his car and his home during that week, but anxieties were rising within him that he was unable to quell without a drink.

A month after the car episode an accident occurred while Joe was watching his son Alex play on a swing set in their backyard. It was a Sunday morning and Alex had been climbing the ladder that led to the top of the slide when he lost his balance and fell backwards to the ground. The ground was soft, but Alex seemed dazed. Joe carried him to his car and rushed the child to the emergency room of the local hospital where he was diagnosed with a mild concussion and released after several hours of observation. Alex was back to normal the following day, but Joe continued to blame himself for his own carelessness and preoccupation which he felt had led to the accident. At this point, Joe began increasing his drinking. Day after day he bought a pint of scotch and binged by himself in his garage. During the month of August Joe took care of his parents' garden and lawn when they went on vacation. This chore was something he had done since he was twelve, and the task had its own history of conflict. One day he went into his parents' refrigerator searching for something cold to drink and found a quart of sour mix. He quickly converted it into scotch sours. Joe was later discovered by his wife having passed out on the kitchen floor of his parents' house. After this event he entered a rehabilitation center and stayed there three weeks.

The Meaning of Anxiety

An alcoholic has been described as a person on fire who runs into the ocean to put out the fire but who ends up drowning. Joe can be viewed as a man living under a great deal of stress who began to "self-medicate" with alcohol. In a sense, the alcohol was being used as an anti-anxiety drug or an analgesic.

Anxiety is present in all of us, but in some families it becomes so intense that it produces substance abuse or other symptoms in its members. Freud and the early thinkers in the field of psychology believed that anxiety resided within the mind and body of the individual. Bowen saw anxiety as part and parcel of the family as a whole that is "absorbed" to varying degrees by its members.

Harriet Lerner sees anxiety as the unresolved emotional intensity that gets handed down to us in our families from the unmourned losses, family secrets and emotional cutoffs from our present generation and from generations past. And Michael Kerr in an article titled "Chronic Anxiety and Defining a Self" explains how he sees anxiety being generated:

> Chronic anxiety, which is assumed to have manifestations on levels ranging from intracellular systems to societal processes, is influenced by many things, but is not caused by any one thing. Whereas specific events or issues are usually the principal generators of acute anxiety, *the principal generators of chronic anxiety are people's reactions to a disturbance in the balance of a relationship system.* Real or anticipated events, such as retire-

ment or a child's leaving home, may initially disturb or threaten the balance of a family system, but once the balance is disturbed, chronic anxiety is propagated more by people's reactions to the disturbance than by reactions to the event itself.

Evaluating Joe's case, it became clear to me that he was carrying a great deal of baggage from his family's emotional past. His family history disclosed that he was genetically predisposed to becoming an alcoholic having that illness on both sides of his family tree. But as I continued to work with Joe I wondered what else brought on his illness at this point in his life.

The two incidents that he had described to me in our first sessions had been extremely stressful if not traumatic, but I was not convinced that his son's accident and the episode with the violent client explained all of the intensity in his life. According to Joe, before he began his alcoholic binging his marriage had been going well and he was a devoted father to his son.

He had career plans that involved a possible promotion and he was taking courses toward a degree in accounting. It was only after I explored what was going on between Joe and members of his first family that I began to understand a major source of the anxiety in his life.

The Critical Father

As Joe began to describe his father, Anthony, to me, a picture emerged of a man who was incapable of showing appreciation or affection. Anthony fit the pattern of the Critical Father whose approval Joe had always sought but was never able to get. Marvin Allen in his book, *In the Company of Men*, offers a description of the Critical Father:

> One of a father's many responsibilities is to help his son
> learn to master his environment. He sets ideals for his son and
> gives him the support and reassurance he needs to attain them.

But the Critical Father sets standards his son can never reach. . . .

Another failing of the Critical Father is that he teaches by pointing out mistakes rather than by highlighting success.
Instead of being mentor and guide, he is judge and critic.

Joe's father not only withheld approval from his son, he also had trouble admitting when he was wrong. The only time that Joe could recall hearing an apology from his father was after an incident involving great emotional pain. When Joe was about nineteen and attending college he continued to mow his parents' lawn as he had done since he was twelve. Each time, his father inevitably found something wrong with the way his son had done the job. On this day the old lawn mower that Joe had been using for years finally broke down, and he decided to replace it with the little money that he had. Joe was able to scrape together one hundred and twenty-nine dollars to buy a gas-powered model from Sears, but when his father saw it in the garage he looked annoyed rather than pleased and said, "I never buy power tools at Sears. I was looking to buy a Snapper."

At the time, Joe felt that he was choking on suppressed rage. If he had been a little boy he would have run away crying, but he was almost a man and felt that he had to endure the pain. Father and son glared at each other and Joe ended up as he always did after a confrontation with his father—in the kitchen commiserating with his mother.

Joe's mother was the peacemaker in the family, as well as her husband's "enabler" in other ways. After his father's tirades she would calm down her son. However, in not taking a stronger position, she was in effect defending her husband. She never seemed willing to stand up to him, but maybe she had been taught that this was something that she as a woman was not supposed to do. She was not always able to relieve her son's pain and when the pressure became too great for Joe he would slam the door and leave the house.

Loyalty Binds

As Joe became older, he defied his father and on occasion even yelled back at the older man when he was being unusually difficult or withholding.

When Joe spoke to me about the continuing conflicts within his family of origin it was clear that Joe saw himself as very different from his father, and in many ways he was. Unlike his father, he spent a great deal of time with his son and he was able to listen to his son's problems in a non-critical manner. However, in other ways Joe had remained remarkably loyal to his father's way and the family "alliances" that his father had made.

"Alliances" is a good word to describe the relationship patterns in Joe's family. His is a family rife with cutoffs—people who have stopped speaking with one another. There is an unspoken rule that you are being disloyal to one family member if you communicate with a relative who has been cut off. The king of the emotional cutoffs was Joe's father. He was at the center of a network of allegiance to his unwritten laws. As I constructed a family genogram with Joe the family alliances and cutoffs became graphically clear. (In the genogram below, cutoffs are represented by a broken line: —— / / ——.)

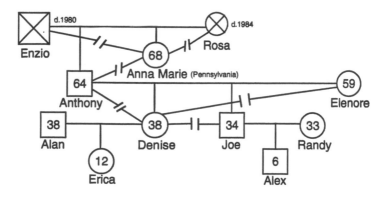

The most striking features of the family's genogram are the number of cutoffs between family members and how the pattern has repeated itself in succeeding generations.

In the same way that Joe's grandmother and grandfather had a cutoff between themselves and their daughter when they were alive, Joe's mother and father are also cut off from their daughter. When I asked Joe if he knew why the cutoff had occurred between his aunt and his grandparents he told me that his aunt had married an Irishman. This was unacceptable to her parents. After that marriage her mother is reputed to have said, "My daughter is dead." The unresolved emotional intensity of this cut off is still reverberating in the next generation of the family.

Joe's father, Anthony, remained faithful to his parents by having no relationship with his older sister. In turn, Joe also cut off from his older sister. When I asked if he knew how the rifts with his sister happened, he related incidents such as missed birthday parties or what appeared to be minor family conflicts. I told Joe if he wished to understand more about what was going on between himself and his sister in the present it might help him to learn more about what transpired between family members in the past.

The Importance of Understanding Triangles

It was virtually impossible for Joe to get a handle on current feelings and behavior within his family without a better understanding of its "triangles." When tensions increase between any two people in a family there is a strong tendency to involve a third party. The process is often automatic and unconscious. Each time things heated up between Joe and his father, Joe's mother became triangled in to decrease the tensions between father and son.

Observe your own behavior when tensions are rising between you and someone else. The impetus to speak about your conflict with another person is often very strong. It decreases the tension between the original two-some by "shifting" the anxiety among three people. The reason that marriage counseling often initially reduces the tensions between a couple is that it creates a triangle with the therapist as the third "side."

In his book *Family Evaluation*, Michael Kerr explains that family triangles are emotional configurations that get passed along from one generation to the next:

> Triangles are forever, at least in families. Once the emotional circuitry of a triangle is in place, it usually outlives the people who participate in it. If one member of the triangle dies, another person usually replaces him. The actors come and go, but the play lives on through the generations. Children may act out a conflict that was never resolved between their great-grandparents.

If we look back at Joe's family genogram, the triangles and the "actors" and "actresses" in each generation become more apparent.

Joe's sister occupies the same position on a family triangle between her mother and father that her aunt did a generation earlier. One could predict that the sister's daughter might be slated to play the same role as her mother and her aunt because of the unresolved emotional intensity that is being passed along to her. When I asked Joe if he knew anything about his niece he mentioned that he had heard that she was having panic attacks. I wondered if this was also the product of the emotional cutoffs that are rampant in this family.

Coaching Joe involved a process called *detriangling*, in which he attempts to establish one-to-one relationships with each member of his extended family. This is a particularly important process for Joe since the loyalty binds of his family demand that he remain cut off from members whom he needs to make contact with.

> *If Joe is able to be disloyal to the way his family has functioned and sustain his right to have relationships with relatives independent of their conflicts with other members, then he will go a long way toward defining a self. But in order to be successful he will have to sustain his new position in the face of powerful family injunctions that he "turn back."*

The family responses to Joe's attempts at change were predictably harsh. He had to control his own reactivity so as not to cut off from others as his anxiety rose.

The following is a segment from a session that Joe had with me in which I was encouraging him to consider reestablishing contact with his sister.

COACH: How long has it been since you spoke with your sister?

JOE: About four years ago she had a major blowup with my dad. I'm not even sure what it was about, but I'm not surprised it happened. If you do anything he doesn't agree with he'll give you the cold shoulder for months. She probably just got fed up with him.

COACH: You just told me what went on between your father and your sister. What about you and she?

JOE: At the same time she stopped speaking to my father she also stopped speaking to me. I tried to contact her but she wouldn't answer any of my messages and when I would finally get through to her she would just hang up. I finally gave up.

COACH: She obviously sees you and your father on the same side. Does she have any reason to think this way?

JOE: I can't think of anything I did to promote this. I remember being really close with her when we were kids. We used to take sides against dad.

COACH: Have you considered writing a letter to her?

JOE: I never have. Would you suggest that I do?

COACH: If you were to write to her it would have to be crystal clear that this is your wish to contact her and that you represent yourself and no one else in your family. My sense is that she will be suspicious and believe that you're trying to contact her on behalf of your parents.

JOE: You're right. I'm sure that she would believe that Mom and Dad are behind any move I make to reach her.

COACH: The other thing to think about is what kind of reaction your father will have when he finds out that you've contacted someone he's written off. It's important that you anticipate his reaction so that you can decide how you'll respond to him. Remember—if and when you do this is entirely up to you. Just thinking about how family members are likely to respond is an important part of this type of work.

At this point in his therapy there were many problems and questions for Joe to resolve in order to attain a new self within the torturous terrain of his family's emotional field. Among the things to evaluate were the costs and benefits of attempting to establish an independent relationship with his sister. Joe's father would probably cut off from him because of what he would predictably construe as a betrayal. But if Joe were to remain loyal to his father by merely going along with his agenda would he be risking never growing up? Would he remain the little, resentful boy forever yelling at his father and then running into the kitchen to be soothed by his mother?

Joe continued to think about his dilemma and the consequences of the decisions that he would eventually have to make. They were critical decisions that would impact on his level of anxiety, his recovery from alcohol dependence and the emotional legacy that he will leave to the next generation of his family.

Examining Our Own Loyalty Issues

Like Joe, most of us are living out our lives while remaining loyal to certain persons, principles and roles from our first families. Some of these feelings and behaviors may be apparent to us, while others may be so ingrained and so pervasive that we are not even aware of the family ritual that we are reenacting. When what we are doing is brought to our attention it may appear to us that we are doing things "dad's way" or "mom's way," but such behavior may be better understood as the way that family members have acted towards each other over many generations and in many different situations.

Sometimes, feelings of guilt can be a signal to us that we are being disloyal to someone or some way of doing things in our families. They may also be letting us know that we need to challenge the system in order to establish a more autonomous position. A son who remains overly loyal to his mother and her unmet needs will be encumbered in meeting his obligations to his wife. "The more rigid the original loyalty system, the more severe is the challenge for the individual: Whom do you choose, me, him, or her?"

Ivan Boszormenyi-Nagy, in *Invisible Loyalties*, presents some of the transitions of loyalty that occur when a new family comes into being.

1. Young parents have to shift their loyalty from their families of origin toward each other; they now owe each other sexual fidelity and nurturance. They have also become a team to produce offspring.
2. They owe a redefined loyalty to their families of origin and to their national, cultural, and religious backgrounds and values.
3. They owe loyalty to children born out of their relationship.
4. Children owe a redefined loyalty to their parents and to the older generation.

Coming from one's mother's family of origin are loyalty issues that involve presenting the family to the world in the best possible light. In many families, bringing up the negatives—family problems, emotional conflicts or anger between members—is not welcome and may be construed as disloyalty to a system with a strong requirement about doing what is proper and right. In my own family I first believed this to be my mother's "personality trait" until I spoke to my first cousin. She related to me that her father—my mother's older brother—had communicated the same message about keeping up family appearances to her.

The following questions may be helpful in exploring your own family loyalty issues and binds:

1. Are there requests that come from my first family that I would not even consider saying No to? What in my family would make me feel extremely guilty if I did not go along with it?
2. Are there things that I do for one adult family member that are done at the request of another member? For example, am I someone who is always responsible for driving my brother places, but he never seems to ask for himself and my parents just expect that I do this?

3. Are there people in my extended family whom I would never think of contacting because I have a sense that someone else in the family wouldn't like it if I did?

4. Are there people whom I expect my wife, children or others to have little or no contact with because of my feelings towards them? How would I feel or react if others decided to make contact or establish more of a relationship with these persons?

First Family Work

Joe has continued to work with me over the past year, and he has been able to make significant gains in extricating himself from his family's loyalty binds. Our most recent sessions have followed the death of his father from a sudden heart attack. It was only after the funeral that Joe was finally able to bridge the cut-off with his older sister, Denise. He mentioned that his mother was becoming too old to manage her house and was planning to move into a home for the elderly. I asked Joe who else was helping with the move and it turned out that he had been planning to pack and organize the transfer by himself. I mentioned to Joe his older sister who was now living in another state. I asked if he had considered enlisting her help in the process. This led to a discussion of his position in the family while he was growing up and the "caretaker" role he seemed always to have played in relationship to his mother. The fact that he hadn't even considered asking his sister's help pointed to a family pattern that probably had not changed over the course of his life. In thinking about Joe's compliant behaviors followed by his angry outbursts, I realized that his relationship to his sister and his mother was worthy of further examination.

Laura Markowitz, an author who writes about families, has described siblings as "peers who share not only the same family, but the same history and culture." When Joe spoke to me about his elder sister, I soon realized that he was describing his childhood protector, the person he had turned to with his early problems. Her concern for him had certainly filled in some of the blank spaces when his parents' conflicts overshadowed their children's needs. Denise is four years older than Joe, and she was always a phase ahead of him as they grew up. I encouraged Joe to begin speaking with his sister on a regular basis. Later he learned that her emotional experiences of early family life were remarkably similar to his.

Joe's reconnection with his sister as an adult has involved "comparing notes" about what happened during their childhood. She is the only person who can confirm some of Joe's hazier memories of family events. She was also able to provide him with the perspective of one who was older when an event occurred. Denise "absorbed" a great deal of the family anger. She also feels it well up inside of her in much the same way that Joe does. Joe was surprised to learn that she also had difficulty with anger since he had always seen her as "outside" the family turmoil in which he so often dwelt. However, I was not surprised to hear that Denise also had repressed anger. It has become clear to me, as a coach, that no matter how distant a family member may appear to be from the locus of distress they will not escape the emotional shock waves that reverberate through the system.

Taking New Positions

The family "scripts" that we have been given as children are often carried into our adult lives. If we are able to change the way we play certain roles in our first family, the other parts of our lives will be easy to work on by comparison.

The way that Joe played his "caretaker" role with his mother over the course of his life had contributed to his feelings of being taken advantage of. It also left him feeling resentful about the normal adult demands made on him by his wife. As a child, Joe knew far too much about the details of his mother's life. Now he's begun to understand how he had been occupying the space of a father who absented himself from his family in significant ways. The family desperately needed a husband and father and Joe was the one scripted to fill the emotional void. The family pattern that Joe and I discussed was a very old one that had existed among Joe, his mother, and his sister for as long as he could remember. When his sister moved out of state Joe was left to occupy this position alone.

Family geography may indicate a great deal about our emotional reactivity to family. Our attempts to feel more comfortable are often revealed by living closer or farther apart. But physical distance or proximity will never resolve the underlying issues or the intensity between family members themselves.

My coaching of Joe involved helping him to consider a different position with his sister that involved sustaining his positive feelings toward her while he also requested her help. Joe had always expressed his outrage after he felt taken advantage of. He was not sure whether he would be able to ask for something from someone whom he cared about without coloring his assertion with anger.

However, Joe resolved that he would not take care of his mother's move entirely by himself and that he would ask his sister for her help. When Joe first suggested to Denise that she might come and help with the sorting and packing of the accumulation of their mother's belongings she reacted with astonishment:

"I'm all the way across the country on the west coast. I've had to do a great deal to help my mother-in-law who has needed my help since she moved into my area."

Joe's sister did not react the way she did to his request

because she is not a helpful person. She was responding to his demand for a change in the way the family had always operated that also challenged her outside position in the system. Following his conversation I encouraged Joe to write a letter explaining how it would be virtually impossible for him to do all the work involved in moving their mother by himself, and that it might be a good experience for both of them as sister and brother to do this project together.

Joe wrote the following letter with my assistance:

Dear Denise,

I've really enjoyed our recent conversations in which we've both been open about our reactions to many things.

One thing that does concern me is your reaction to my request that you participate with me in the packing for Mom's move.

Very practically, it would be quite difficult for my wife and me to bear the entire burden of packing all of the accumulated items that Mom needs to move to her new residence. Even with much given away and thrown away it is a monumental task. There may be several days of packing, and Mom does not have the strength to do it by herself. I've had to work overtime three nights a week and Sue works at the flea market on weekends. I have taken a number of sick days from work to shuttle Mom back and forth to visit the program, meet with administrators and sign the lease. My sick days are valuable and limited and I am running out of them. I am glad to do my part but it has also been emotionally taxing at times. I understand that your living in another state does not allow you to be a part of all that goes into Mom's transportation and care but I do feel that my request for your involvement in this move should be honored.

Sometimes when I am relating what I have been doing regarding Mom you will bring up what you have been doing for your mother-in-law. I can appreciate all that you have done for her but it hasn't helped me or our family. I realize that you find it difficult to deal with Mom but it is also difficult for me at times—and what if I also decided that I'm just not up to taking care of her?

What you may not be looking at is that this is the home that we both grew up in and packing up and saying our "goodbyes" together may benefit both of us. And since neither of us are "only children" neither of us should have to do a task like this alone. And I am asking for your help.

Love,
Joe

Denise flew in and worked for a solid week on the sorting of the accumulation of a lifetime of household items and the packing of what was going to be moved to their mother's new apartment. Denise and Joe also got to spend some important time alone in which they talked about how they had once been close but had completely lost touch for long periods of their lives.

To the casual observer not that much had happened in the weeks preceding Joe's mother's move to her new home. A brother asked his older sister to help with an elderly mother's move and she agreed. But in the family system of which Joe was a part significant changes had taken place:

- Joe had been able to ask for help directly in a family with a history of indirect communication where anger was the only medium of exchange.

- Joe had been able to step out of his role as sole caretaker of his mother by enlisting his sister's participation with him as a peer.

- By working together on this project Denise and Joe were able to reestablish their family relationship as siblings who share a common history in a house they were both "saying goodbye to."

- By remaining calm through the emotional turmoil during this period Joe was able to enhance his adult position in his family. He had successfully "updated" his sister about who he is now, in contrast to the angry, impulsive boy that she remembered from her childhood.

16

TOWARD A
NEW FATHERHOOD

W HAT WILL IT TAKE, on a personal and a political level, to create a new concept of fatherhood? How can we invest fatherhood with a new significance that will overcome our second class position and make us relevant to our families? The attitudes that we carry tend to reinforce the behaviors that we most need to change, and the cues that remind us of our diminished status are everywhere.

I was sitting in a playground watching a father with his children. He was actively involved in their play, helping his daughter walk across a suspended wooden bridge that swayed slightly. His son, a toddler, was seated a few feet away in a sandbox with a plastic shovel in his hand. The father kept an eye on his son's movements as he attended to his daughter's need for physical support and encouragement. A woman pushing a stroller with a sleeping three-year-old stopped in front of the father and smiled.

"I see you're baby-sitting today," she said. On the surface the woman's comment appeared friendly and inconsequential, but actually her remark cut to the heart of society's perception of fathers. If a woman is with her children doing any of a multitude of activities, she is viewed as performing her expected role as mother. When a man is with his children, he is "just baby-sitting."

The Second Parent

As fathers, we are not seen as primary caretakers. A father with a baby in his arms may be viewed as "cute," but he is not taken seriously. He is expected to become frazzled if the baby starts to cry and then hand the child back to its mother. The television image of the ineffectual father is pervasive, and the bumbling fools of the sitcoms continue to be the images of a father that most children witness through adulthood.

A father with his children is generally seen as the second parent who is engaged in a holding action until the primary parent takes over. He is rarely seen as a man performing a vital family role with his children.

The second class status of fathers as parents is a self-perpetuating myth that feeds upon itself. As a society, we have blamed men for not participating in their children's lives, but we have offered them little in the way of social support that would help them to change their role. Inequities in the legal system reinforce a father's inferior position in child custody cases. Furthermore, fathers who have refused to pay child support are portrayed as criminals regardless of their circumstances or reasons for non-payment and consequently become the targets of politicians who like to show that they are aggressive on this issue.

Track Them Down and Make Them Pay!

There is no doubt the Deadbeat Dad is someone who should be forced to pay his share of the cost of raising the children he has brought into the world. However, something has gone awry when one of these men makes the cover of *Newsweek* with his head framed by a WANTED poster for an article titled: "Deadbeat Dads: Wanted for Failure to Pay Child Support."

What has been overlooked in our zeal to extract payment from delinquent fathers is that these men have also abandoned their families emotionally. All that our society demands from them is they pay what they owe financially. By labeling a father a criminal and not even examining what else is behind his reasons for abandoning his family aren't we, once again, only looking at fathers as breadwinners while ignoring their importance in other areas?

David Blanckenhorn, in *Fatherless America*, sees the focus on getting Deadbeat Dads to make payments as an avoidance of the deeper father losses we have suffered as a society:

> In our cultural model of the Deadbeat Dad, the core issue is money absence, not father absence. . . .We do not ask this guy to be a father. . . . We ask him to send a check. Our prevailing understanding of these guys simply misses the point. For children and society, the decisive question is not whether men will pay child support, but whether men will be fathers. For what is broken in our society is not the proper police procedures to compel small child support payments from reluctant men. What is broken is fatherhood.

Finding Our Voice

We are not living in a "father friendly" society. Some of the unfriendliness that is directed against fathers has to do with the fact that fathers are a very large social group without a voice. We have no national magazine or organization. There are no lobbyists in the halls of Congress making sure that the interests of fathers are fairly represented. We also have no leaders or spokesmen that reporters can call to get our position on issues that are relevant to us. We are the silent sons who grew up watching strong, silent "heroes" on television and movie screens. Media heroes became our role models who taught us to mask our pain and not complain about it. Our silence, however, has taken its toll on our health. And the stresses of growing up become evident when we consider the following facts:

- Men die earlier than women in every major disease category.

- The death rate from cancer is one and a half times greater for men than for women. The death rate from heart disease is twice as high for men as women.

- Men commit suicide between two and three times more often than women.

- Men are ten times as likely to commit suicide after the death of a spouse.

- Men are four times more likely than women to be the victims of murder.

- Men, on the average, live seven years less than women.

Where are the commissions to study why men are so at risk? Why is so little being done to help a group that is in a mental and physical health crisis? Also, shouldn't research be conducted at this moment to understand the socialization of boys that prepares them for high stress professions?

It becomes clear as we examine the facts that a campaign to change the male role should be in place before the major male stressors take their toll on this generation.

Author and feminist Harriet Goldhor Lerner clearly states in her book, *The Dance of Intimacy*, what women have needed to do in regards to their plight in society. Her message can be further applied to the situation that men and fathers are experiencing:

If we did not clarify our own needs, define the terms of our own lives, take action on our own behalf, no one else would do it for us. Feminists began busily writing women back into language and history establishing countless programs and services central to women's lives. And new scholarly journals and women's studies programs appeared in universities to name just a few actions. Only in response to changing our own selves and to taking individual and collective action on our own behalf would men be called upon to change.

The women's movement has made tremendous strides in the past thirty years in establishing greater equality for women. Leaders have also encouraged fathers to be partners in parenting, so that mothers can develop their own careers. The one thing that the women's movement cannot do is represent fathers or speak for men.

The theory that women, as a group, are oppressed while men, as a group, are their oppressors has led to a greater awareness and study of women's issues while men's concerns have received little attention. Due to the absence of a vocal men's movement that can promote the idea that men's problems are *also* socially caused, men in many instances are portrayed as criminals and perpetrators. Consequently, the roots of men's problems continue to be ignored. When men are viewed as a distinct social group that has a voice and political power, men's issues and father's rights can become the subjects of discussion and study just as women's problems have.

Taking a Stand and Changing Ourselves

Whether we are looking at individuals in families or groups in society, the change process is similar. Bowen's theory can be applied to either. As fathers living in families, we do not grow emotionally or develop new skills simply because our wives are making efforts to improve themselves. *All meaningful change involves changing ourselves.* In the same vein, men in general and fathers in particular will not benefit themselves or their wives by just doing the laundry and being supportive of women's rights. We are a group that has been socially isolated in a breadwinner role for many generations. Thus, we need to join with other men to assume new positions in family and community life.

There are certain predictable reactions to our attempts to bring about change. They are the "Change back!" responses that occur whenever an individual or a group initiates a significant new way of doing things. Several years ago, I became tired of being in charge of family finances. Over the years, I had become the primary breadwinner, the bill payer, the budgeter, and the checkbook balancer. I had also become the one who worried over money as well as the one who felt blamed if there wasn't enough money for the family vacation we had been looking forward to or the new car that we badly needed. I felt both my wife and I had gotten used to a system in which I *overfunctioned* in the area of money management and she *underfunctioned*. For a period of time in our marriage, she felt "taken care of" while I felt competent and in control. As time went on, I began to also feel overburdened and she was unable to participate equally in family decisions, since only I knew how our money was being spent. I felt this needed to change. My wife should be informed about family finances and become an equal partner in this area. Gradually, but not without friction, things changed.

Our will and our resistance to change will probably coexist forever. This is true whether we are talking about the way a couple manages its money or the role a father plays in the lives of his children. Change will always produce anxiety which, in turn, will bring about pressures to return to "the old way of doing things."

The principle of maintaining new positions in the face of other people's pressure on us to "turn back" is a universal formula for change. If we do not cut off from others at this time, everyone will take a step forward.

The Fatherhood of the Future

The search for a new concept of fatherhood is part of society's broader dissatisfaction with aspects of contemporary marriage and family life. However, fathers and families live their lives in the day to day world of schools, communities, and the workplace. Meaningful changes in family functioning will only occur if the larger network of institutions accommodates family needs. When fathers' rights organizations started to call for fairness in child custody decisions and a respect for paternity in the workplace, the courts began to change their attitudes. As a result, the right to paternity leave became the law of the land. In the United States, organizations such as The Fatherhood Project and The National Congress for Men and Children have begun to study fatherhood and "reunite" fathers with their children. (See the appendix for more information on organizations that support fathers' involvement with their children.)

Our social policies are only as progressive as our prevailing attitudes, and the search for a new fatherhood may involve some profound changes in the way we see the world.

I envision four major areas of change that would allow for the creation of a new fatherhood in a new society:

1. SEEKING HELP IN FATHERING NEEDS TO BE
   VIEWED AS NORMAL. There is presently no stigma in
   going to the doctor's office, whereas there is a wall of
   secrecy that surrounds the need for counseling. The idea
   that families occasionally react to stress and change with

some type of emotional symptom will be considered "normal." And going to get "coaching" will be thought about the same way we consider going in for a physical checkup today. A future society will look back at our era as the "Age of Secrecy" in which people devoted a lot of energy to hiding their problems from one another. It will be considered a virtue to talk openly about what is going on in one's life so that we can all learn from each other's problems.

2. FATHERS NEED TO LEARN TO REMOVE THEIR "GENDER JACKET." In our future society men will learn to adjust to new demands. They will learn to emphasize cooperation over competition, see the family's growth to be as important as occupational growth, and value the maintenance of relationships as much as they value their self-reliance and independence. After several generations, it will probably be found that men can adapt to the skills required by the new society as well as their female counterparts, and they will realize that they had just been the victims of behaviors and attitudes which were passed along to them from past generations.

3. LEARNING ABOUT FAMILY AND RELATIONSHIPS NEEDS TO BE A LIFELONG PROCESS. In the new society of the future, children will, during kindergarten, begin to learn the rudiments of family life and relationships. School curricula in this future society will continue to teach basic skills and preparation for technical careers, but children will also learn how to get along with others and how to build meaningful relationships. Society will have come to understand that it is meaningless to just accumulate technical knowledge if an individual does not know how to manage his relationships with others. The primary value of the society will be to produce people who are able to sustain long,

intimate relationships with each other. Other acquisitions will have become less important to this society as a whole. An individual in this society will be expected to be extremely knowledgeable about his own lineage and the family system of which he is a part. It will be understood that many of the problems that people experience have to do with patterns that have existed before in their family histories. Having a working knowledge of how your family operates emotionally will have become as commonplace as knowing how to spell.

4. OLDER ADULTS MUST BE SEEN AND UTILIZED AS IMPORTANT "RESOURCES." In the ideal society of the future, the grandparent generation will no longer be a group without an important role. They will be viewed as very valuable repositories of family knowledge and history, and they will be expected to spend time with their grandchildren, telling the family stories and recounting their understanding of past and present family events.

Bringing It All Back Home

Of all the societal changes that we have contemplated, none will contribute more to the development of stronger identity for a father than learning more about his own father's life and the emotional system in which they both have a part.

In my opinion, the approach to change called "coaching" along with the pioneering work of Murray Bowen on the family is a relatively new area of study with tremendous potential for the future. During my last five years as a family counselor and coach, I have found the stories of my clients' personal growth almost always involve taking a step back into the past to speak to family members with whom the client has lost touch or become cut off from. I am frequently impressed by the courage and creativity of my clients as they embark on this reconnection and gain understanding and take new positions with wives, friends, parents, siblings, and other important people in their lives.

For most of my life, I had believed that my original family was the cause of the problems I had. This was what I had learned in therapy, and the notion was reflected in the therapy that I did with my clients. I have since come to understand that every member of my family, including my parents, is a part of an emotional process that has filtered through the generations, and that everyone—including myself—has a responsibility to grow as much as possible within that system. If I were to blame my parents and hold them responsible for my growing up, I could spend my life searching for someone to give me what I felt I "never got." However, if I am able to let go of the idea that my parents are "supposed" to have done something "the right way," then truly I have the potential to change. Understanding more about the emotional history of my family and being objective enough to "observe" my own participation in the process can do more to help me become the man and the father that I want to be than anything else I might do.

I have come to see my reconnection to my past as a bridge. The bridge that I have constructed in my mind connects me to my father's generation and the generations of the family that preceded him. When I stand on this bridge, I am able to see a broader family panorama than I have ever seen before. I see a link between what came before me and what I am trying to create.

17

Q & A:
COACHING AND
DEFINING A SELF

THE PRECEDING CHAPTERS HAVE provided an outline of family of origin "therapy." For many, this is a new way of looking at changing relationships and oneself. Questions will arise about how the process called "differentiation" takes place, the time and effort required to do this work, and some of the problems people encounter in the process.

Some are inclined to see this work as self-help and "go it alone" while others may wish to enlist the services of a coach. In either case it is worthwhile examining the advantages and disadvantages of each approach.

The following suggestions cover some of the issues that commonly arise when people consider this method of change.

1. *The process of "differentiation" or "defining a self" seems to involve being able to think clearly and not allow one's feelings to determine one's reactions. Doesn't this move people away from feelings that they need to be "in touch" with?*

All people have within them a feeling and a thinking part. During calm times family members and others are usually able to think more clearly and not just react to feelings that are constantly being set off. During a crisis when anxiety is higher it becomes more difficult for each of us to think about our emotions and remain aware of our own reactions. The goal of *differentiation* is to stay "in touch" with our feelings and yet not allow feelings to control us. It is about keeping the thinking brain working during times of high anxiety and emotional turmoil in our marriages, families and work situations. When we can do this we move in the direction of greater differentiation. When we cannot think, we are simply being *reactive*. This is not about denying or avoiding feelings but about being aware and able to think about feelings at the same time. People who can only feel and are unable to think about their feelings are at a distinct disadvantage in relationships and life in general.

A woman whom I was seeing in counseling was about to marry her third abusive, alcoholic husband. When I asked why she thought she was doing this she could only talk about her "love" for him. Since she was not able to think about her feelings and what had happened before, her reactivity would pull her into another self-destructive relationship.

2. *Can I become "too differentiated?"*

When people ask if they can become "too differentiated" they generally are asking, "Can I become too distant from others?"

The process of differentiation means that you are becoming clear about who you are. Using differentiation, you can begin to have closer relationships with those important people in your life than you were able to have before. This might include members of your first family and your partner.

Differentiation implies the ability to be intimate—to make clear statements about who you are and to allow others to do the same.

3. *How long does the process of differentiation usually take?*

I believe that differentiation is a process that goes on over the course of our entire lives. As children we move in the direction of individuation—becoming more of an individual with a distinct identity. Differentiation is the adult process of "returning" to the system from which we came and defining our own identity with members of our first family.

The approach to change described in this book is about accelerated and focused family of origin work that involves gathering information and taking new positions with significant people from our emotional past. The process usually takes several years and people tend to work at their own pace. It cannot be done quickly because change stirs up a great deal of anxiety in families that have operated in the same ways over many generations.

4. *Why can't I just work on differentiating, or defining a self with my partner? Why do I need to include my mother and father in the process?*

We can work on defining a self in all areas of our lives, and our marriages are certainly significant areas in which to establish intimacy and take clear positions on important issues.

Bowen Theory and some research in the field have shown that maximum growth will occur when an individual is able to establish one-to-one relationships with each member of his extended family. Parents and siblings are the most important people with whom to establish an adult relationship in a new way. Many of the ideas about who we are come from how we saw and still see our parents. A change in the way we see them will often create a change in the way we perceive and experience ourselves—and this changed sense of self tends to carry over into other relationships in our lives. The capability to observe our own participation in our relationship with our parents is a powerful change technique.

5. *I realize that I'm not doing this work to try to change my mother or father, but I keep feeling that nothing different is happening when I spend time with them.*

It is true that significant change is always about changing ourselves. The more we try to get others to change, the more we became trapped in our own resentments and reactivity. We don't get to change our parents, but we can take clear, well-thought out positions with them. After that we need to step back and realize that we cannot control how they react to our new positions. We can decide to stick to our position in the face of pressure to change back and we can remain calm enough to not overreact when we don't get the response we want. The process that I just described will bring about change—not necessarily in our parents but in ourselves.

For over a year, I worked with a client named Hank around a lifelong problem that he had with his mother. Hank wanted a closer relationship with her and calmer family gatherings. His mother would become angry and cut off from family members when she became anxious. Hank's mother made few changes in the basic way she handled situations during the year that I saw him. Hank, on the other hand, made significant emotional changes within himself by remaining calm enough to observe how he responded to his mother's emotional episodes and by not cutting off from her as he once used to do. Emotional growth sometimes occurs in subtle ways, but never when we insist that others must change. When we are able to relinquish the position that others must change, change will sometimes occur.

6. *Is it possible to do family of origin work if one or both of my parents have died or if there are very few living relatives?*

My own father died more than twenty-five years ago and yet I've done a great deal of work on my relationship with my father and my family of origin. If a father or other family member has died, a person investigating his original family can learn about his father by speaking with other family members who were emotionally connected to him. When a person spends time with a relative who was important in his father's life he enters what is called his "emotional field." When I was speaking to an aunt and a cousin who knew my father I began to have vivid memories of him.

Things that I had forgotten came to life again after not thinking about him for many years. The emotional "system" that my cousins grew up in was very similar to mine. We have the same grandparents and both of our fathers also grew up together. The patterns of behavior and emotion were clearly similar once we began to talk openly about ourselves and our families.

7. *I feel that my parents are people who were abusive to me when I was a child and I find that they continue to treat me poorly as an adult. What purpose would it serve for me to reconnect with them now?*

If we are able to keep in mind that we're not doing this work for anyone else but ourselves it becomes easier to justify our attempts to reestablish ties with our parents. The "purpose" or goal of reconnecting with family members is still differentiation whether a parent is remembered as caring or abusive. If a parent has been abusive, it is almost predictable that people in that family will be very reactive to one another.

The goal of the work is not to confront a parent or have an emotional scene: that usually creates defensiveness and nothing new is learned from the encounter. Being able to return to the abusing parent and maintain a degree of objectivity in his presence will be a significant, empowering move for an individual to make. As adults we are able to set limits on what others can do to us which we were unable to do as children.

8. *Sometimes I find myself slipping into old patterns when I spend time with my parents. What can I do to avoid my old behaviors?*

Visiting with parents and other family members requires some strategic planning. The idea that this time we will return home and have a wonderful time with our parents is a fantasy that many of us hold onto. Often, our parents will say or do something that will push our buttons and we will react in the same way we did when we were nine or eleven or fifteen years old. We need to predict what our parents or siblings will do and decide how we're going to respond. Planning short, manageable visits rather than long ones can allow us to remain clearheaded, objective, and less reactive to what will go on.

9. *I try to get my parents to speak about their lives but they don't want to. What should I do?*

Sometimes we are trying to get out parents to speak about their past lives in order to unearth the emotional issues that our parents grew up with, and they may not feel comfortable revealing these memories. It can be just as fruitful to ask factual questions about the details of their lives—who shared a bedroom and who came to holiday dinners. Whatever our parents tell us about themselves and their families reveals important things about the emotional life of their families, their values and their beliefs.

10. *I visited my father with the desire to break through his wall of silence. I confronted him with the truth but he just turned me away.*

You will be more successful in this type of work if you move toward small manageable changes. Emotional scenes and confrontations usually produce more reactivity with little new understanding. The purpose of speaking to one's father or mother is not to have an encounter session or a "love in"—but to adopt a new position in which you may learn something about yourself and the emotional system of which you are a part.

11. *I approached my mother last week but she was only willing to talk about my sister's miscarriage, not my issues. Was she just avoiding me and should I have pressed my issues?*

There is no point to bringing up your issues when your family is in crisis and emotional turmoil. Try to bring up issues again during a calmer period.

12. *Whenever I try to spend time alone with my father my mother is always there. What can I do about this?*

Fathers often rely on their wives to handle their relationships with their children. Try not to blame either of them, but be aware that you may have to create a plan to spend time with him alone. This type of thinking about how the family operates is part of developing a clearer picture of your own participation in what is going on.

13. *I'm twenty years old and in college but still living in my parents' house and being supported by them. Can I still do family of origin work?*

It is difficult to establish new positions with people on whom we depend economically. However, it is still possible to take the research position and learn more about the lives Of members of your extended family.

14. *I find myself getting involved in conflicts with my wife's family. Is it possible to work on my own issues with them?*

If a person wants to work on another person's relationships he is usually avoiding working on the ones in his own family.

Our partners need to work on their own relationships in

their families. They need to differentiate and define who they are in that emotional arena. We can be more helpful when we step back and limit our involvement in what is going on between the partner and her original family. We need to be clear in our relationships with our partner's family members, but the deeper issues that exist there are never ours.

15. *The goal of defining more of a self sounds a lot like other therapies. Is family of origin work really different from conventional psychotherapy?*

In most therapies, the client explores feelings and does much of his important work with the therapist. Coaching involves working with a client so that he will be able to speak directly to members of his family in a new way. Coaching involves standing on the sidelines and offering a client strategies and suggestions on how he can make important moves in his marriage and family of origin. In coaching, the most important work goes on outside of the therapist's office. We differentiate as we are able to be more intimate and take new positions with the important people in our lives.

16. *What are some of the specific advantages of working with a coach over approaching this as a self-help activity?*

One of the main advantages of working with a coach has to do with the intensity of the feelings that inevitably get stirred up when we try to change behavior patterns in our families. As easy as it may be for us to remain calm and objective in other situations, it is virtually impossible not to lose our focus when we try to reconnect with important people from our past. This is because our emotional attachments to these central figures in our lives are never fully resolved. Since the coach is not part of our family, he can retain his objectivity and keep us on track when we begin to overreact.

For men who are accustomed to working alone, it can be a learning experience to work cooperatively with someone on a "project" that involves both thinking and feeling.

17. *Are there any advantages to approaching this as self-help work and not using the services of a coach?*

There is an advantage to thinking independently and keeping your own counsel since that fosters defining who you are in your family which is the goal of this work. We all need to be ready to get some coaching when we lose our objectivity in the intense emotional field of our relationships.

18. *What might a professional therapist who has been trained to do family of origin work be able to do that a friend or a men's group could not offer?*

A professional coach who does Bowen family therapy has been trained to think about families differently than most laymen and some therapists. He or she will be more familiar with the patterns of behavior that go on in families and how they are passed from one generation to the next. The professional coach will also be able to create a genogram with you—a three generational family diagram that explains the emotional connections between people in your family and other significant issues. His strategies will probably be more sophisticated than the suggestions and support that you might receive from a men's group or a friend with whom you are working.

19. *Can a woman be a coach for a man or is it best for men to coach other men?*

There is no reason that only men should coach other men or that a woman cannot be an excellent coach to a man. In my opinion, the appeal for many men in working with another man is the association of being coached with a sports technique and not by therapy. Many men don't like the idea of going to see a therapist but the strategic approach of coaching appeals to them. It includes some of the traditional skills that men were taught as they grew up.

20. *Can my wife act as my coach?*

One person who would not make an effective coach would be a spouse. A person who is emotionally involved with both you and your family would be unable to sustain an objective position on what you would be trying to accomplish.

21. *I only see myself doing the work described in this book with a professional therapist. Can this book still be helpful to me?*

The first step in the direction of change involves thinking differently about an issue or a problem. Since we have all been trained to believe that emotional problems exist inside a person, it may take some flexibility to consider the central idea of this book, that problems are interactional and go on between people. This book is designed to provide a father with a new approach to working on family problems.

APPENDIX

Constructing a Family Map

The process of going back to fathers, mothers, and other relatives to gain knowledge and a new perspective on family and self can be a challenging task. The genogram is a family tree that tracks a family's emotional connections as well as its births, deaths, marriages, and divorces. It is an important tool in the coaching process. It reveals the family patterns that repeat themselves from one generation to the next and it lends understanding to one's own place in the larger system.

The following genogram simply shows my relationships to my extended family.

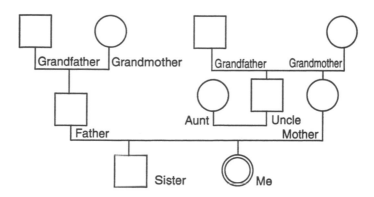

The following are the key symbols and lines:

SYMBOLS	LINES
☐ MALE	⌐⌐ MARRIED COUPLE
○ FEMALE	⌐⌐ SEPERATED COUPLE
☐ ○ COUPLE CONNCTED BY MARITAL LINE	⌐⌐ DIVORCED COUPLE
☐ ○ INDEX SYBOL (PERSON DOING GENOGRAM)	⌐ ⌐ UNMARRIED COUPLE
☒ ⊗ DECESACED MALE AND FEMALE	

Family maps show marriages, indicated by connecting horizontal lines:

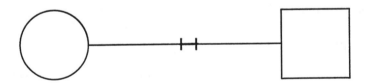

Divorces are shown as breaks in those lines:

It also tells you when someone has died:

And which children came out of which marriages:

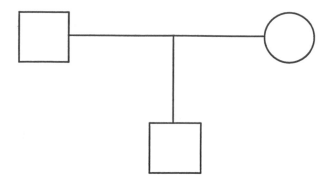

What makes the genogram more instructive than the family tree is that it includes other information such as occupations, behavior patterns, and relationship histories.

In the words of Emily Merlin, President of the New York Association for Marriage and Family Therapy:

> The genogram is a road map of your family. It will show you where you came from and where you are going. If you study the road map, you'll get to know the "territory"—the people, places, and events that make up your history.

The genogram can also be used to examine family patterns or themes. When I became interested in the topic of fatherhood, I also wanted to learn more about the problems that men in my extended family had with anger. When I interviewed family members and constructed my family genogram, I learned which men had anger problems and noted it on my diagram. The pattern of violence between fathers and sons became highlighted as I tracked it through the generations on my genogram.

Other family themes that can be better understood by placing them on this three generational diagram are jealousy, extramarital affairs, alcoholism, conflicts, secrets, medical problems, or any issue that seems to be a pattern in family members over time. The genogram can help you to see your connection to people in your family and the issues that go on between them.

Whenever I see an individual or a couple for counseling, I begin by taking their history and placing the information that they give me on a genogram.

During my first session with the Townsends (below), I began by constructing a simple genogram that includes only husband, wife, and child. Later, I will include their families of origin, also. Our initial dialogue is presented on the left-hand side of the page, while the stages of genogram construction are shown on the right:

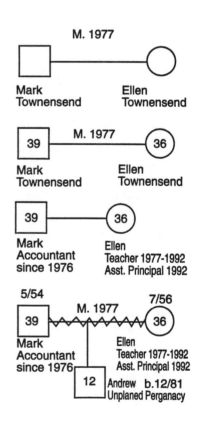

Mr. Townsend: Ellen and I met in December of 1975. We dated for one-and-a-half years and were married in March of 1977.

Coach: How old are each of you now?

Mr. Townsend: I was thirty-nine in April. Ellen will be thirty-seven in July.

Coach: What jobs have you and Ellen held over the years?

Mr. Townsend: I've been an accountant since 1976, and Ellen was a teacher since we married until last year. She became an assistant principal.

Coach: When did you and Ellen first think about having children?

Mr. Townsend: Actually, Ellen began pushing for children two years after we got married. We started arguing at that point. Andrew was not a planned pregnancy. He was born in December of 1981.

Counseling Centers

The centers listed below use an approach to counseling that includes coaching and family of origin work. They will often make referrals to other counselors or centers that may be out of their city or even out of state.

> The Ackerman Institute
> 149 East 78th Street
> New York, NY 10021
> (212) 879-4900

> The Center for Family Consultation
> 820 Davis Street Suite 221
> Evanston, IL
> (847) 475-1221

> The Family Institute of New Jersey
> 312 Amboy Avenue
> Metuchen, NJ 08840
> (908) 548-0444

> The Family Institute of Westchester
> 147 Archer Avenue
> Mount Vernon, NY 10550
> (914) 699-4300

> The Georgetown Family Center
> 4400 MacArthur Boulevard NW
> Suite 103
> Washington, D.C. 20007
> (202) 965-0730

The George Hall Center
600 East Mall Third Floor
Etobicoke, Ontario M9B4B1
(416) 622-8833

The Minneapolis Institute of Family Dynamics
6950 France Avenue S
Suite 119
Minneapolis, MN 55435
(612) 927-5499

The Princeton Family Center
14 Vandeventer Avenue
Princeton, NJ 08542
(609) 683-4188

Western Pennsylvania Family Center
733 North Highland Avenue
Pittsburgh, PA 15206
(412) 362-2295

Fathers' Rights Organizations

Listed below are two Father's Rights Organizations that provide information and advice to fathers about child custody and other issues.

Fathers' Rights and Equality Exchange
701 Welch Road #323
Palo Alto, CA 94304
(500) FOR-DADS
(415) 853-6877

Fathers for Equal Rights
P.O. Box 010847
Flagler Station
Miami, FL 33101
(305) 895-6351
(305) 895-7461

Other Resources for Divorced Fathers

The Official Parents Without Partners Sourcebook
By Stephen Atlas
Running Press, 1984

The Parents' Book About Divorce
By Richard A. Gardner
Bantam, 1982

Organizations: Fathers and Children

The organizations listed below support greater involvement between fathers and children. James Levine and The Fatherhood Project have become a clearinghouse and networking center for information on fatherhood and other men's issues:

The Fatherhood Project Families and Work Institute
330 Seventh Avenue
New York, NY 10001
(212) 465-2044
    Contact: James A. Levine

The National Congress for Men and Children
2020 Pennsylvania Avenue
Suite 277
Washington, D.C. 20003
(202) FATHERS

Men's Issues Think Tank
4839 305th Avenue NE
Cambridge, MN 55008
(612) 689-5885
Contact: Lowell Johnson

Tapes and Books

For tapes and books from Jane Myers Drew, call:

(800) 950-DADS

Or write to:

Tiger Lily Press
P.O. Box 15277
Newport Beach, CA 92659

REFERENCES

Allen, Marvin. *In the Company of Men*. New York: Random House, 1993.

Blankenhorn, David. *Fatherless America*. New York: Basic Books, 1995.

Bly, Robert. *Iron John*. New York: Addison-Wesley Publishing Company, Inc., 1990.

Boszormenyi-Nagy, Ivan. *Invisible Loyalties*. New York: Brunner Mazel, 1984.

Bowen, Murray. *Family Therapy in Clinical Practice*. Northvale, New Jersey: Jason Aaronson Inc., 1978.

Cary, Sylvia. *The Alcoholic Man*. New York: Lowell House, 1991.

Carter, Elizabeth and McGoldrick, Monica, eds. "The Family with Adolescents." In *The Family Life Cycle*, pp. 147-169. New York: Gardiner Press, 1980.

_____. "Family Therapy with One Person and the Family Therapist's Own Family." In *Family Therapy*, edited by Philip J. Guerin, pp. 193-219. New York: Gardiner Press, 1976.

Coleman, Arthur D., and Coleman, Libby Lee. *The Father*. New York: Avon, 1988.

Drew, Jane Myers. *Where Were You When I Needed You Dad?* Newport Beach, CA: Tiger Lily Publishing, 1992.

Erikson, Erik. *Childhood and Society*. New York: W.W. Norton and Co., 1963.

Griswold, Robert L. *Fatherhood in America*. New York: Basic Books, 1993.

Kellogg, Terry. *Grieving and the Process of Recovery*. Deerfield Beach, FL: Health Communications Audio-Book Series, 1991.

Kerr, Michael E. "Chronic Anxiety and Defining a Self." *The Atlantic*, September 1988, p.47.

Kerr, Michael E. and Bowen, Murray. *Family Evaluation*. New York: W.W. Norton and Co., 1988.

Kramer vs. Kramer. Columbia Pictures, 1979.

Lerner, Harriet Goldhor. *The Dance of Intimacy*. New York: Harper and Row, 1989.

Levenson, Daniel J. *The Seasons of a Man's Life*. New York: Random House, 1978.

Lidz, Theodore. *The Person*. New York: Basic Books, 1968.

Markowitz, Laura. "Shared Passages." *The Family Therapy Networker*, 1994, pp. 28-29. Silver Spring, MD: 1994.

Marlin, Emily. *Genograms*. New York: Contemporary Books, 1989.

References

National Center of Health Statistics. Washington, D.C.: U.S. Department of Health and Human Services, 1982-1994.

Papp, Peggy. "The Godfather." *The Family Therapy Networker,* May/June 1988, pp. 49-52.

Pasick, Robert. *Awakening from the Deep Sleep.* San Francisco: Harper Collins, 1992.

Pittman, Frank S. *Man Enough.* New York: G.P. Putnam Sons, 1993.

Pruett, Kyle D. *The Nurturing Father.* New York: Warner Books, 1987.

Richardson, Ronald. *Family Ties That Bind.* Vancouver, Canada: International Self-Counsel Press Ltd., 1984.

_____. "Playing Your Own Tune in the Family." Audio Tape, AAMFT Conference. Decatur, GA: The Resource Link, 1988.

Schnarch, David M. *Constructing the Sexual Crucible.* New York: W.W. Norton and Co., 1991.

Shapiro, Jerroid Lee. *The Measure of a Man.* New York: Delacorte Press, 1993.

Thompson, Keith. "What Men Really Want: An Interview with Robert Bly." In *New Men, New Minds* by Franklin Abbott. Freedom, CA: The Crossing Press, 1987.

Waldman, Steven. "Deadbeat Dads." *Newsweek,* May 4, 1992.

Wallerstein, Judith S., and Blakeslee, Sandra. *Second Chances.* New York: Ticknor & Fields, 1989.

Zilbergeld, Bernie. *The New Male Sexuality.* New York: 1992.